SUPERNATURAL
ENCOUNTERS

ISBN-13: 9781671547889

A Publication of Tall Pine Books
|| tallpinebooks.com

SUPERNATURAL ENCOUNTERS

REAL STORIES OF A TRUE BELIEVER

TIM GRISHAM

Tall Pine

DEDICATION

I dedicate this book first and foremost to my wife, Peggy, who has stood with me in faith, prayed for me, believed in me and loved me with the love of God unlike anyone else except Jesus.

And to all those who have *and continue* to support this ministry; many now for *thirty plus years!*

CONTENTS

AUTHOR'S NOTE

The stories you're about to read are true and have been written from my own memory and personal documentation. It was not my purpose to write my experiences in a chronological order, but in a way I felt would best interest those reading this book. Some of these events took place more than thirty-five years ago and some more recent. My desire is to follow up with a second book *Supernatural Encounters 2*.

If this book blesses you and encourages you, please take time to communicate the effects of this book by emailing me at TGM12345@aol.com. Your comments will be greatly appreciated!

—*Tim Grisham*

INTRODUCTION

This book is a compilation of many years of personal encounters that I have had with Jesus and the power of the Holy Spirit working in and through my life. Many accounts of witnessing, winning souls, healing the sick, and other miraculous signs have happened outside the four walls of the church. It has been my experience that many Christians go looking for the power of God, signs, wonders, and miracles *inside* the church. There is a time and purpose for these manifestations to work in the church. However, God wants us as believers to take His Word outside the four walls and watch Him work with us and confirm the Word with signs following.

> "And they went out and preached everywhere, the Lord working with them and confirming the word through the accompanying signs. Amen." (Mark 16:20 NKJV)

The Great Commission, as it is most commonly referred to in the Gospels of Matthew, Mark and Luke, is not the "Great Suggestion," as some would like to think of it.

"And he said unto them, Go ye into all the world, and preach the gospel to every creature. He that believeth and is baptized shall be saved; but he that believeth not shall be damned. And these signs shall follow them that believe; In my name shall they cast out devils; they shall speak with new tongues; They shall take up serpents; and if they drink any deadly thing, it shall not hurt them; they shall lay hands on the sick, and they shall recover." (Mark 16:15-18 KJV)

Notice that this is not just written to His disciples at the time, but also to those who would believe in Him. As believers, we have been given a mandate to "go ye" with a promise that God would work with us confirming His word with signs following. As you read through these encounters, know that it is God by the power of the Holy Spirit who did these things. It is not because of a special gift or anointing that others do not have.

Though I am called by God to be an evangelist and graced with the anointing to carry out that call, it does not give me something extra when it comes to sharing Christ with others. The gift of the evangelist is a gift given to the Church for the equipping of the saints for the work of the ministry as found in Ephesians 4:11. I encourage every believer in Jesus Christ who has received the gift of the Holy Spirit—according to Acts 1:8, having been filled with the Holy Ghost and power—to step out and let God work through you!

The purpose of writing this book is to share with you my transition from being a person who was saved with a desire to do something for God; to a person saved and being used by God to impact the lives of people, unlike anything I had imagined at that time in my life.

GETTING OUT OF THE BOAT

MY FIRST STEPS IN MINISTRY

IT WAS 1983 and I was attending Bible school in Fort Worth, Texas. My greatest desire at the time was to work for Jerry Savelle, a well-known Bible teacher, and to be around other believers of like precious faith. I remember one day complaining to the Lord and telling Him how I felt that it was a waste of my time to work a secular job in the construction industry. The world was going to hell and I was stuck working a job I did not enjoy! I felt I should be preaching to other Christians about how they needed to go into the world and tell others about Jesus.

You see the irony here, right? I am one of those Christians who is in the world, where people are dying and headed to hell, but don't see the forest from the trees! Honestly, I felt that because I was going to Bible school, my time would be better spent working in a "Christian" environment and telling others what they needed to do.

It is important for me to be honest about where I was spiritually during that time in my Christian life. I did not know much; I knew very little about the Bible and how the kingdom of God operated. In fact, the Lord did not deliver me from my secular job of working construction while attending Bible School. He did quite the opposite. God clearly spoke to me and said, "Tim, if you do not change your attitude about your job and begin viewing it as your ministry, you will never have a ministry." When I heard this in my heart, I remember thinking that *God was testing me to see how bad I really wanted to be in full time ministry.*

As I looked back a few years later, I realized first and foremost that God has called every believer to be full-time ministers of reconciliation. Second Corinthians 5:18 says, *"Now all things are of God, who has reconciled us to Himself through Jesus Christ, and has given us the ministry of reconciliation."* If you believe you are a new creation in Christ according to 2 Corinthians 5:17, then continue reading through the next couple of verses and you will discover the powerful truth: as a new creation in Christ, you are also God's minister of reconciliation!

The idea of being a minister, *not* because I was going to Bible School to earn a diploma or because I was working to be recognized by a Christian organization and receive ordination, was a hard concept at the time. I felt that I needed man's recognition and man's approval. It is not bad to have man's recognition or man's approval; however, it must be secondary to knowing we are first and foremost God's workmanship and that what God says about us far outweighs what man says or thinks. Don't get me wrong, I am thankful for the recognition I have been given by other ministers and ministries and how they trust me as a faithful minister of the Gospel; however, we must believe God's word first over man's.

"For we are His workmanship, created in Christ Jesus for good works, which God prepared beforehand that we should walk in them." (Ephesians 2:10 NKJV)

Once I began to believe the Bible and what God said about me, I began changing my attitude about work. Realizing that it was not just a job that I dreaded to get up and go do in the mornings, but, rather, an opportunity for ministry, my life changed drastically!

DALTON'S CORNER 1982

While in my first year of Bible School, Peggy and I attended a church called The Stepping Stone in Burleson, Texas. It was there that I met two guys who would have a profound impact on my life. Ken and Gary were the kind of Christians who I thought of as a little off. You know, those people who are extremely excited about Jesus and continually say, "Praise the Lord!" These guys were real fanatics for Jesus. I considered myself as much more conservative and a "normal" Christian.

Ken and Gary not only attended the same church, but the same Bible school I was attending. They would always come to school with stories of how they had been out on the streets over the weekend sharing Jesus with people, not only seeing others get saved but also healed, delivered, and all kinds of other exciting things the Lord was doing. God was doing these things through them.

Actually, it sounded to me as somewhat of an exaggeration on their part and nothing that I felt God was calling me to do. Regardless, it still seemed to capture my attention. See, I felt God had called me to be a preacher to the church. My desire was to preach like Jerry Savelle or Kenneth Copeland, in large auditoriums and at big crusades around the world. My desire was not to stand on a street corner and preach to people, who, in my opinion, could not care less. Little did I know how much I was about to learn!

For many weeks, Ken and Gary invited me to go with them on Saturday nights to share Jesus with people at a place called Dalton's Corner. Dalton's Corner was a multi-level nightclub, and on each level, a different style of music was played: Country, Rock, and Disco. A variety of people were drawn to the nightclub and these people did not always get along well, especially after a few drinks under their belts. For weeks, I declined their invitation to go out preaching on the streets—especially to some nightclub. After hearing the stories week after week, my interest was finally piqued. Even though Ken and Gary were a tad too fanatical for my liking, I finally agreed to go out one Saturday night with them.

I remember arriving at Dalton's Corner. People were everywhere! Most were sitting in the parking lot drinking beer and enjoying themselves. It was a flashback to a time just a few years prior, when Peggy and I had been doing the same exact thing on a Saturday night. I remember thinking that these people were not there to hear about Jesus; they were there to party. I had the idea that if people *wanted* to hear about Jesus, they would go to church, like I did. I realized that this idea was an excuse. In my mind, there were more churches than there were people who could fill them and there was plenty of room. I also had the opinion that if someone wanted to hear about Jesus, they could simply turn on their television and turn to twenty-four hour a day Christian broadcasting. I had it all figured out. With the technology that God had given man at that time, there was really no reason for me to go out into the streets or especially some bar or nightclub and tell people about Jesus!

We parked the car and both Ken and Gary jumped out of the car with this excitement that I didn't understand while I sat there gripped by fear. They called out, "Come on, let's go," but I just sat there. In fact, I locked the doors of the car and told them I was staying there to pray for them. They could not convince me to get out of the car, so they left me sitting there.

Upon their return a couple of hours later, they were even more excited. I recall them saying, "You should have gone with us. You really missed it!" They began sharing stories of the things God had done and how they were able to pray with people. My heart was hungry for these kinds of experiences, but my flesh was weak and my mind fearful. When I got home that night and got ready to go to bed, all I could think about was that I should have stepped out and gone with them. I made a commitment to myself that the next time they asked me to go —not sure that they would—I would go and not stay behind.

The very next week, as they normally did, Ken and Gary were making plans to go back to Dalton's Corner. This time, I asked if I could go with them. Their reply was, "Sure, but not if you're going to sit in the car all night." I promised them that I wasn't going to sit in the car all night and I was going to go with them.

The time came all too quickly and I found myself in the same spot. Arriving in the parking lot of Dalton's Corner, once again, I felt fear rising up within me and my imagination going wild. Before I knew it, Ken and Gary were out of the car and headed to the nightclub. I got out of the car and began walking to catch up, but somehow lost them in a crowd of people gathered around the other side of the building. I stopped right in front of the entrance thinking to myself, *Lord, what do I do?*

As I turned to go back to the car, I saw a car load of people parked near where I was standing. I heard the Holy Spirit say, "Go tell those people about Me." My mind was racing with thoughts of fear and doubt. I stepped off the sidewalk and went right up to the driver's side window of the car. The guy behind the wheel rolled down his window; smoke and the smell of marijuana and cigarettes came rolling out. The guy said, "Hey man, you want something?" I quickly counted five people in the car, two in the front and three in the back seat. My mind seemed to be blank as how to respond. Again, I thought, *What do I say, Lord?* Then I opened my mouth and replied, "Yes, I want to tell you about Jesus and how He loves you and wants to come into your life."

Laughter followed from those in the car, as though it was a joke or something, but I felt and sensed something in me for the first time unlike any other time. The anointing of Jesus rose up within me and I could feel the power of God coming up out of me; the Word of God began flowing like a river. To this day, I cannot remember everything I spoke to those people, but as I began speaking the Word of God, a hush came over that car load of people and they listened to me as I shared the things the Lord gave me to say. I can still remember their faces as the Holy Spirit did not speak condemnation or hell and damnation to them, but the pure love of God.

I don't know how long I was there or how long they listened to me, but in the end, I asked, "Would you like to pray with me and invite Jesus to come into your life to save you and give you the gift of eternal life?" At that moment, I felt as though I was back to myself and the anointing that I felt had subsided. All five of the people in the car said yes to receiving Jesus! I know that what I felt was not something that came from me, but it was the Holy Spirit in me, manifesting through me.

"Make up your minds beforehand not to worry about how you will defend yourselves, because I will give you such words and wisdom that none of your enemies will be able to refute or contradict what you say." (Luke 21:14-15 GNB)

That night changed my life. I realized that the "Greater One" (1 John 4:4) lived in me, and His anointing was not just something that we will feel from time to time, but it is His person living in us, His power and His love. That night, Ken and Gary were not the only ones with a story! I, too, had a testimony of God's power working through me in a way that I had never experienced before. I went home with a joy unspeakable and full of glory. I remember telling Peggy, "Honey, you should have been there. It was awesome!"

I will always be grateful to the Lord and to Ken and Gary for their encouragement. It is amazing how God can use others to encourage you to step out into the ministry He has given to us all. I pray that this book of my life encounters will encourage you in the same manner, to take that step of faith. Get out of the boat and step onto the waters of life, trusting God's Word to uphold you and make you a witness and a soul winner for Christ.

2
―――――――――

LIFE OR DEATH?

WHEN PEGGY and I decided to go to Bible School, we left everything we had and moved from Colorado to Texas. My parents, my sister, and my brother also moved to Texas. Times were especially hard in the early eighties. The economy was bad. Additionally, the type of construction business my dad owned and operated was struggling in Colorado due to jobs being few and far between. Texas offered opportunities for new construction and work that gave us all hope. My dad started a construction company and I worked for him during Bible School. My dad even attended some Bible School classes from time to time, and my sister attended school for a time.

In the spring of 1983, we were attending a Sunday night special meeting at our church with guest speaker Jerry Savelle. I remember clearly that during Brother Jerry's message, he stopped and told the church we needed to pray in the Spirit. He went on to explain that our prayers that night were for a life and death situation. As I began to pray, the Lord gave me a vision, and in this vision, I saw faces of people tumbling as though they were in a barrel rolling down a hill. During the vision, I remember that fear tried to come upon me and that I took authority in Jesus' name over that fear. The prayer time did not last long and then Brother Jerry continued with his message.

That night as we left the church, our young daughters Tiffany and Candice wanted to ride home with my parents. At the time, my parents were driving a small compact Toyota pickup with just one bench seat and we decided that the girls wouldn't be able to ride home with them that night. Of course, they did what most little kids do and cried for Grandma and Grandpa. Peggy and I did what many parents do with small children and bribed them with a stop at McDonald's for some french fries. Because we chose to stop at McDonald's, we were running about ten minutes behind my parents. Once the kids were quieted, we were back on the road headed for home to Burleson, which was about a thirty-minute drive from the church where the meeting was held.

After just a few minutes on I35, we saw flashing lights in the distance. It was not unusual to see accidents on the busy Texas freeways. Other than praying for God's help and intervention for those involved, we did not think much of the accident we were approaching. The closer we came to the accident, it was obvious that the accident had just happened. Motorists were pulling off to the side of the road to help and others who weren't paying attention were slamming into each other causing a larger accident.

As we were maneuvering around the mess of vehicles, I glanced over to the right side and noticed a vehicle with an "I Love Jesus" bumper sticker. It was my mom and dad's truck! I pulled off the freeway onto the grassy median and told Peggy to stay there, watch the girls, and pray! My words were, "My God, pray!" I ran to the little blue truck, and as I got closer, fear attempted to grab ahold of me. The little blue truck looked so bad and I kept thinking that there was no way they could have survived. The top of the truck had been completely severed off and thrown away from the vehicle. I had no idea where my parents were and searched frantically for them.

By this time, emergency personnel were on the ground. It was then that I saw my dad lying down in the grass of an embankment. When I got to him, he was gray and had no color. His throat had been cut from ear to ear and blood was pouring out. I placed my hands on him and said, "In the name of Jesus, I command this bleeding to stop. In the name of Jesus, Dad, you are going to live and not die, according to Psalm 118:17, '*I shall not die, but live, And declare the works of the Lord.*'"

Immediately my dad opened his eyes and said, "What happened?" I told him to lay still. I explained to him that he had been in an accident and that Jesus was here to help him. He asked, "Where is your mother?" I told my dad not to worry and told him that she was okay. I spoke to him by faith, as I didn't know if my mom was okay, but knew that God was in control. I had just witnessed the power of God stop my dad's bleeding, bring him back to full consciousness, and give him a voice to speak with his throat cut wide open! I knew I had to find the medics right away. I ran to the medics and explained where my dad was located. They were not aware that there had been another person in the truck.

We learned later that my parents had been ejected out of the truck and had landed 175 feet apart from each other. I also did not know that the medics had pronounced that my mom was dead at the scene. Another person who had stopped to help had come from the same meeting at church. This guy was a new believer and had only been saved a few days. When he saw my mom, he laid hands on her and declared that she was going to live and not die in the name of Jesus. Life came back to my mom's body. The paramedics rushed to work on her as her injuries were very severe. A helicopter transported my mom to the hospital. Stabilized, they loaded my dad in an ambulance and headed for the hospital.

I am sharing this testimony of life because I want you to know that even in death, the power of God can change circumstances. The name of Jesus has the power to heal, the power to raise the dead, and the power to overcome any circumstance. I could write an entire book about this time in my life. My parents both lived through the accident and declared the works of the Lord according to Psalm 118:17. Their healing was instant at times, and at other times, it took months of standing on the Word of God to see it come to pass. Through it all, God was faithful. God is faithful.

We each have to decide what we are going to believe. If we find ourselves in a life and death situation, how are we going to respond? Are we going to fall apart like a cheap pair of shoes, or are we going to believe God's Word and stand in faith, activating the Word of God in our lives? I decided long ago that I am going to believe God and believe His Word. I'm not going to allow my experiences, even when they are contrary to the Word of God, to move me away from my faith. God is good, His Word is true, and it does work in my life.

3

THE MIRACLE OF ANDY

DURING MY YEARS in Bible School, I worked construction with my dad. We had all sorts of characters come to work for us. Some would only work until lunchtime; they would leave for lunch and never return. Others would work for a few days and move on.

One day, a guy named Andy showed up asking for a job. Little did we know that Andy had just been released from jail. Andy was a hard worker, but also hard-hearted. He had a habit of frequently asking me, "What time is it?" After a few days of him asking me and me telling him to go buy a watch, I decided to use this as an opportunity to witness to him. Each time Andy would ask me, "What time is it?" I would tell him, "It's time to get saved!" This went on for a few months. When I would try to witness to Andy and share the Gospel, he resisted.

One day while working on building the fireplace in an apartment complex, things changed. It was about ten minutes until our lunch break and Andy came in. I was sure he was going to ask me the time, but instead he said, "Hey, boss, you know that thing you're always telling me?" At first, I didn't know what he was talking about, so I replied, "What are you talking about?" He said, "You know how you're always telling me to get saved?" It dawned on me that he was referring to our time conversations from the past, so I replied, "Yeah, what about it?" Andy said, "I'm ready." Glory to God! I was so excited to hear him say those words.

I told Andy to go shut down the equipment and I would tell him how to get saved during our lunch break. A few minutes later, I heard a blood curdling scream, the kind that makes the hair on the back of your neck stand up and your heart feel as if it just fell to your stomach, so I dropped my tools and ran as fast I could to where the scream came from. It was Andy. He was standing with his back to me, about a hundred feet away next to the cement mixer. My first thought was that he must have gotten his arm caught in the mixer blades, as his body was shaking. This had happened to another guy and had snapped his forearm.

In response to what I thought was happening, I did what I knew to do first and that was to unplug the electrical cord. As I got closer, I realized that Andy was standing in a puddle of water where the water hose had leaked that day and the electrical connection was laying in the water. Andy was being electrocuted! I reached down, grabbed the extension cord, and jerked it apart.

Andy went flying backwards through the air, almost as if someone had just pushed him as hard as they could. He hit the ground on his back and began going into what looked like a seizure. By this time, other workers had gathered to see what was happening and someone yelled to call the paramedics. Andy's body went as stiff as a board for a few seconds and then went completely limp. It appeared as if he was not breathing. All of this happened in just a few minutes' time.

I got on top of Andy, straddling him, and put my hands on his chest and said, "In the name of Jesus, Andy, you are going to live and not die. I command you, in Jesus' name, be whole and healed!" Then I began speaking in tongues over him. A few minutes passed and I heard the ambulance sirens. The paramedics pushed me aside and went to work. I told them that I thought he had been electrocuted. As they loaded him into the ambulance, I got in my truck with another guy who worked with us and followed the ambulance.

When we arrived at the emergency room, we waited for about twenty minutes, all the while praying in the Spirit. Romans 8:26 NLT says, *"And the Holy Spirit helps us in our weakness. For example, we don't know what God wants us to pray for. But the Holy Spirit prays for us with groanings that cannot be expressed in words."*

A nurse came out to the waiting room and asked me if Andy took drugs. I told her that I didn't know if Andy took drugs. She then asked me if my friend and I were on drugs. I replied, "What are you talking about? I am not on drugs. I am here waiting to see how Andy is!" She told us that the doctor would be out in a minute. I thought to myself, *I guess she thinks we are on drugs because we had been praying in other tongues.*

A few minutes later, the doctor came out to meet me. Like the nurse, he also asked us if Andy was on drugs and asked if we were taking drugs. I was frustrated and a little confused by the questioning. I replied the same way I had replied to the nurse. Then I told the doctor, "Hey, I want to know how Andy is doing. He works for me and I need to know." The doctor replied, "There is nothing wrong with him. I don't know what kind of prank you guys are trying to pull here, but you need to get your friend and leave this hospital!" I was shocked by the way the doctor spoke to us.

He took us to the room in the emergency room where Andy was waiting. Andy was sitting on the bed and I said, "Andy, how are you?" He replied, "What is going on? Why am I here?" I told him everything. I told him that the devil tried to kill him. I explained how he had come to me just before the lunch break to ask about being saved and all the events that followed our conversation which led to us being at the hospital. I told Andy that we were praying before we left the hospital. It was time to ask Jesus into his heart. Andy quickly said yes!

I don't know for sure if Andy was electrocuted; the doctor said there were no burn marks. I don't know if Andy died when his body went limp and he stopped breathing, but I do know when I said "In the name of Jesus, Andy, you are going to live and not die" and then laid my hands on him that he began to breathe again! When he left the emergency room, there was nothing wrong with him. Praise the Lord!

4

MANIFESTED GLORY OF GOD

WHAT IS the glory of God? The Bible describes the glory of the
Lord at times as an all-consuming fire and a cloud. In the book
of Luke, the glory of the Lord shone around them, and in Acts,
Paul saw a great light on the road to Damascus. Isaiah 60:1-2
NKJV is the scriptural precedent for what I am about to share:

> "Arise, shine; For your light has come! And the glory of the
> LORD is risen upon you. For behold, the darkness shall cover
> the earth, And deep darkness the people; But the LORD will
> arise over you, And His glory will be seen upon you." The
> prophet Isaiah says, "And His glory will be seen upon you!"

After the incident with Andy, the story continues. The next
day, one of our other workers came to me and asked if he could
talk to me in private. I agreed and we took an early lunch. We
sat in my truck and I asked him what was going on. He hesitated a bit and then said, "I am not on drugs and I don't see
things and I don't want you to think I am crazy." I listened and
acknowledged what he said.

He continued, "Yesterday, when Andy got hurt and you

were down on the ground over him talking in some language. What were you saying?" I explained to him that I didn't have a clue what was being said and that the language is from the Holy Spirit. I told him that it was a heavenly language.

He sat there for a moment with a strange, and almost fearful, look on his face. What he said next is powerful. "When you were speaking, I saw your hands start to glow white and the white light went up your arms and you began to glow with light. I am not crazy; I am telling you the truth."

I was blown away and excited, but I kept my demeanor and explained what he had seen. "Oh that, that was the Glory of God, His power manifesting through me!" When I prayed over Andy and laid hands on him, I did not see anything or feel anything. I simply did what Jesus said to do: *"Lay hands on the sick and they shall recover."* In Mark 16:17, Jesus said, *"And these signs will follow those who believe."*

I told the worker that God did that as a sign to him that God is real; God is alive and He wants to give him the gift of eternal life through Jesus Christ. I went on to share more of the Gospel with him, which resulted in him praying with me and asking Jesus to be the Lord of his life! I was so excited that he gave his heart to Jesus and excited that someone witnessed the Glory of God manifest through me. It's not up to us to decide when or how the Glory of the Lord is revealed. It is up to us to preach the Word, share the Gospel, and know that the Lord accompanies the Word, with signs following.

> "The disciples went and preached everywhere, and the Lord worked with them and proved that their preaching was true by the miracles that were performed." (Mark 16:20)

Later on, my mind tried to convince me that what this worker saw may have been an exaggeration on his part. Even so, he did give his heart to Christ.

A couple of days later while at work, another worker approached me asking to talk to me. At noon, he met me up in the attic where I was laying brick for a fireplace chimney. He brought up Andy getting hurt and shared with me almost word for word exactly what the other worker had seen. He said he hadn't been able to sleep at night thinking about what he had seen. I explained what he had seen and shared the Gospel path to eternal life with him. He, too, received Jesus that afternoon.

I share these stories not to make myself look super spiritual, but to share examples of the goodness of God and how He desires to show Himself strong to those who believe His Word and are willing to be doers of the Word and not hearers only (see James 1:22). God desires to work through us in ways we could never imagine, all we need to do is believe and proclaim His Word to others.

5

HOW TO GET JOHNNY SAVED

AS I HAVE SHARED ALREADY, God challenged me to change my attitude about working a secular job. I wanted to leave the secular, worldly atmosphere of the construction business and go to work for a Christian ministry that would provide me with a "Spirit-filled work environment." I wanted to separate myself from sinners and any ungodliness; yet, that was not what God had in mind for me. What I needed to realize, and we all need to realize, is that we are the light of the world; we are the ones who carry the light of Christ and the answer to the problems of the world. We are the ones God has chosen to take the greatest news, announced to the world by angels to men, to all the Earth. Yet, these angels did not seek out men of great importance, men of wealth, men of position, or great leaders of world power. God chose people just like me and you to tell the news: shepherds out in a field tending their flocks!

One day, we had a guy by the name of John stop by the job site looking for work. It just so happened that we needed another worker, so we hired him. During this time, I was still attending Bible School in Fort Worth, Texas. John was somewhat of a bragger. He loved talking about how good of a worker he was, and he also talked about his weekends, how he partied or went to some bar and "picked up some chick," as he put it.

Week after week, I started dreading coming to work on Monday because I knew John was going to make it a point to tell me about his ungodly experiences that weekend. I would try to preach to John, but my approach was more condemning him and his sinful lifestyle than talking about the goodness of God. I have learned through experience and Jesus' example that if you approach people in condemnation, they will usually resist anything you have to say.

I prayed and asked the Holy Spirit how I could get through to John. I was tired of hearing about all his ungodly escapades, listening to his dirty jokes and filthy language. The Holy Spirit instructed me to share with John some Bible stories. "Why would he want to listen to Bible stories, Lord?" I heard the Holy Spirit tell me to tell him the "right" stories and he would listen.

It was a Monday morning and John showed up to work ready to tell me all about his weekend exploits. I interrupted John and proceeded to tell him about a guy I knew who had quite the weekend himself. "John, your weekend could not have been anything like this guy I know. He saw this beautiful woman. She was a real knockout. She was naked, outside, taking a bath!" John stopped in his tracks and said, "WHAT? Where was this, who was she, and did you see her?" I had John's attention. I went on to tell him the story of David and Bathsheba, from 2 Samuel 11:2: *"Then it happened one evening that David arose from his bed and walked on the roof of the king's house. And from the roof he saw a woman bathing, and the woman was very beautiful to behold."*

When I finished the story, I explained to John that I had told him a real-life story from the Bible. John said, "No way!" Then I read him a portion from my Bible. From that day on, I told John different stories from the Bible and John would listen. I told him things from Proverbs about the prostitute: *"Stolen water is sweet, and bread eaten in secret is pleasant. But he does not know that the dead are there, that her guests are in the depths of hell"* (Proverbs 9:17-18 NKJV).

John would listen to my stories, however, he still wanted to hold on to his way of life. Every Friday when our shift ended, I would invite him to church on Sunday. John would always laugh and say, "If I walked in the door of your church, the roof would fall in!" He always blew me off with a laugh and some smart remark.

One Friday afternoon, as we were getting ready to leave the job site, I asked John, "John, are you going to go to church with me this Sunday?" And to my surprise, John said yes. I thought he was joking. He said that he had been thinking about what I had been saying and that he would like to try going to church. He said he would only go "just this one time to get you off my back." I was thrilled!

Sunday rolled around and John showed up at the church. He made several cracks about the roof falling in and how he might have to get up and leave in the middle of the service. He wanted to make sure he sat in the back row close to the door. John was sure we would probably be rolling around on the floor and speaking in some crazy language before it was over. He said that when that happened, he was "out of there." I assured him that I had no plan of rolling around on the floor, but if he didn't like being there, he could leave at any time with no problem.

As the service began, it was obvious that John was a fish out of water. He smelled of alcohol and cigarettes. He wasn't a typical churchgoer. He was nervous and uncomfortable. As the music continued and the praises of God elevated, John turned to me and said, "Here we go, they are about to roll on the floor and jump the pews!" I told him to hang tight and that it was going to be ok.

When the music ended, John seemed to relax a bit. Our

pastor, Pastor Harold Nichols, got up and began his message. As was his custom, he told a couple jokes, which seemed to get a smile from John and set him a little more at ease. He finished his jokes and then told the congregation, "Turn in your Bibles to the Gospel of John." I think John was surprised to know that there was a book in the Bible that had his name. The title of the message was, "How to Get Johnny Saved!"

All of a sudden, John turned to me and said, "I can't believe you told your preacher about me! I am out of here!" I quickly told John, "No. I promise I did not tell him anything. He does not know you're here." I convinced John to stay, but as soon as the service was closing, John got up and left.

The next week, I worked to convince John that I had nothing to do with the pastor's message and that he needed to come back to church the following Sunday and give it one more try. By the week's end, John agreed to come one more time.

On Sunday morning, Pastor Harold got up and shared his jokes. He then asked everyone to turn to the Gospel of John. John looked at me as though I had set him up again. Pastor Harold continued with the title of the message, "How to Get Johnny Saved Part Two!" That was it, John was hot. From that day on, I was unable to convince John that I didn't have anything to do with the message that Pastor Harold preached. I tried to tell him that it was God speaking to him; however, he wouldn't listen to me.

I continued to witness to John over the next year and eventually John left to take a different job. I always felt like maybe I did not do enough to reach John. I felt that I had somehow failed God, but I continued to pray for laborers to be sent across his path.

"Therefore pray the Lord of the harvest to send out laborers into His harvest." (Matthew 9:38 NKJV)

Ten years later, my parents attended a Benny Hinn conference in Tulsa, Oklahoma. After one of the services, my dad heard someone calling his name from the crowd. My dad's name is John, and someone was yelling, "Hey, John, John Grisham!" My dad said he turned to see who was calling out to him. It was John, the same John who had worked for us years ago and who I had spent a year witnessing to.

My parents were shocked to see John at a Benny Hinn meeting. He told them he had gotten saved finally and was on fire for the Lord. He asked my dad how I was doing. My dad told him I was well and in the ministry. John told my dad, "Please tell Tim that I never forgot the things he told me. Because of all those Bible stories and you all witnessing to me, it pointed me in the right direction and I finally received the Lord just a year ago!"

It became so real to me then that we should never judge whether our testimony and witness has made a difference in someone's life. We do not know the impact we are having on others. Paul said in I Corinthians 3:7 NLT, "*It's not important who does the planting, or who does the watering. What's important is that God makes the seed grow.*" Jesus spoke about the sower and how you and I are sowers of the Word of God. God's Word is the seed of Life! I learned not to ever discount the power of God's Word when sown into the heart of a person.

6

HEARING GOD ONE STEP AT A TIME

AFTER GRADUATING Bible School and receiving my ordination from Calvary Cathedral International in Fort Worth, Texas, in 1984, Peggy and I—along with our two daughters at the time, Tiffany and Candice—moved back to Penrose, Colorado. We really believed in our hearts that God wanted us to go back and bring the Word that we had learned about faith. He wanted us to go back and share how God loves us and desires to bless us and to give us life and life more abundantly. I did not know how to do it, but as we obeyed God, and the direction we felt He was leading us in, we believed He would show us.

We started a Bible study as soon as we were moved back to Penrose. Only two besides us attended: my mother-in-law Pauline and my sister-in-law Alley. For the first few months, it was just the four of us and our two daughters. We had such a blessed time sharing the Word of God together and eventually we started Living Word Outreach from that Bible study. I will share more details on that experience later.

In 1987, we merged Living Word Outreach with another church in a nearby town and stepped out into the ministry of the evangelist. From 1987 to 1989, I was on staff with a church in Pueblo, Colorado, as the Staff Evangelist and to oversee the outreach ministry for the church. There was no outreach to oversee, so it became my job to create it. The truth is that I spent more time fixing things at the church than working on the church outreach ministry. During this time in my life, I learned that my ministry did not begin-and-end based on a church position. God called me, He anointed me, and it was up to me to "go ye" into all the world. The position I held at the church turned out to be for my good, in that I learned how to keep a right attitude even when others did not treat me right.

Over the two-and-a-half years I was on staff, I would go out to the streets every Friday and Saturday night to witness to the young people hanging out downtown and to the drunks and party goers at the bars and nightclubs. I did not do these things because it was my job; I did these things because I was called to. I did them on my own time after putting in forty plus hours at the church and working every Saturday doing construction to supplement my salary. There were many nights that I felt exhausted when I headed to the streets to minister and I would have rather gone to bed and gotten some rest. However, I resisted how I felt and did what I believed God was leading me to do. Except for the times that I traveled overseas to minister or preached out of town, I maintained this rigorous schedule from 1988 to 1994.

It wasn't long before I had several guys who would join with me in street ministry. And after a couple of years, I had other pastors of different churches asking me if they could send people to go with me to the streets. Of course, I said yes to whoever wanted to be part of the growing street outreach ministry I had started. This was the beginning of what God had called me to do: equip the Church for the work of the ministry according to Ephesians 4:11. I will share more about this in later chapters.

7

DEVIL IN THE DARKNESS

ONE SATURDAY NIGHT, while walking the streets of Pueblo, I encountered a young guy dressed all in black. My impression was that he was dressed in the punk rock style with a long black leather coat and spiked hair. At the time, I was in my early thirties and had my own long hair styled in a mullet. To give you more of a visual, my hair was long and curly in the back and short on the sides, and I had one side of my head shaved with a big cross. I was no punk, but I certainly had my own style going on.

I approached the man in black to give him one of the Gospel tracts. As I went to hand it to him, he opened his coat and grabbed his black T-shirt by the neck and ripped it right open! When he did this, he growled at me, snarling like a wild animal. Tattooed on his chest was a satanic symbol. He yelled loudly, asking if I saw his tattoo. I think he thought I was going to run in fear. I said, "Yeah, I see that. Looks like a ticket to Hell, but I am here to give you a ticket to Heaven."

He looked at me as though I was the one growling and acting like an animal. He turned and ran as fast as he could in the other direction screaming. I followed him as fast as I could, yelling that Jesus loves him and to not let the devil kill him but to let Jesus save him. Eventually, he outran me into the darkness. This man was demon-possessed. I don't know what became of him, but he heard from me that Jesus loved him. I showed the devil that night that I was not going to be intimidated. I also did what the scriptures say: Submit to God, resist the devil, and he will flee!

8

MINISTRY IN THE STATE MENTAL HOSPITAL

THE MAN in black was not my only encounter with demon-possessed people. For several years, I visited the Colorado State Hospital for the mentally ill and spent time ministering to the guys in maximum security.

I remember this man named John M. John, a convicted child molester who had attempted to kill a person. When I met John, he was in maximum security. John talked about God, but he had a perverted view of God. I would visit John on a weekly basis. After a year of sharing the Word of God with John and giving him reading assignments in the Bible, John was showing a lot of progress. The hospital began to lower his medications and even asked to have a meeting with me regarding John. In the meeting, I was questioned by five doctors and some of the hospital staff for about an hour. They wanted to know what I was telling John and what I believed about God. When the meeting ended, the head doctor asked me to continue to counsel only John; I agreed to continue.

After another year of counsel, John was moved to minimum security with on-grounds privileges. This meant that John could go on the grounds of the hospital without supervision for a couple hours a day. John was getting ahold of God's Word and it was changing him! One day, I got a call from the hospital asking if I would be interested in taking John to church. Praise God! The only condition was that I was responsible for picking him up and bringing him back on time. I agreed and John attended church with me the next week.

Over a period of several years, I ministered to John. I led him to salvation and the baptism in the Holy Ghost. John was moving toward being released from the hospital. Eventually, John was moved into a half-way house with minimal supervision. John witnessed to many others in the state hospital and would regularly introduce me to other patients, some who were even worse off than John. My ministry to some of the patients continued via long distance phone calls after moving out of Colorado in 1994. I will never forget my ministry to John and how God impacted his life and my life. I continued to grow and I learned that no one is beyond God's help and that the Word of God is able to set the captives free!

Not every case ended like John's. There was a man named Greg, who believed he was Jesus and that he was going to come on a white horse and bring vengeance on everyone. I met Greg when one of the hospital staff asked if I would be interested in talking to a guy in the max ward. I, of course, I agreed. However, I'm not sure what the intentions of the hospital staff were and it's possible that they wanted to see how I would handle Greg.

Greg was not going to be released from the hospital. Greg had a lot of mental problems; he had attempted to kill his mother and had been pronounced insane. However, I knew that if a demon possessed man who lived in a cemetery, who cut himself and was bound with chains only to break free, could be set free by Jesus in the Bible, then Greg had a chance, as well.

Greg made it as far as giving his life to Christ and realizing he was not Jesus. He was moved to a different floor of maximum security and was given TV privileges and contact with other patients. I spent many hours sharing the Word of God with Greg. There were times when it seemed he was going backward, but then it would turn around and I would see hope.

I never saw Greg leave the hospital in the years I ministered to him, but I watched God's Word change him into a man that received Jesus as Savior. A man who was not possessed by the devil, thinking he was Jesus Christ, and into a person who desired to know Jesus more and more. No one is beyond God's reach!

If you can get someone to listen to the Word of God, and listen long enough, it will penetrate. The Word is what holds the power to set people free, no matter what the problem is. Don't let the devil or anyone else try to convince you there is no hope for people, because that just is not true. The Bible gives us numerous examples of people who were set free by the power of Jesus Christ.

You and I are Christ's ambassadors. According to 2 Corinthians 5:20, *"Now then, we are ambassadors for Christ, as though God were pleading through us: we implore you on Christ's behalf, be reconciled to God."* And verse 19 says, God *"has committed to us the word of reconciliation."* The Word is the key to releasing the power of God in people's lives; it's not prayer that sets people free, it's the Word of God! Jesus said in John 8:32, *"And you shall know the truth, and the truth shall make you free."* Preach the Word, teach the Word, speak the Word, share the Word, and watch what the Word of God will do in your life and the lives of others!

9

GAS STATION GOSPEL

EVERY WEEKEND, I would meet with seven guys to pray and then go to the streets to witness. One night, I pulled my car into a local convenience store to get some gas. At the store I pulled into, there was a push button on a call box to tell the cashier how much gas was needed and how the person was going to pay for the gas. This was before you could pay at the pump. I asked one of the guys with me to take my payment into the store while I was filling my tank. The store was full of people and I could see this friend of mine waiting in line.

The attendant had left the little speaker box on and I could hear the conversation inside the store. I knew that the attendant and everyone inside the store could hear me, as well. I decided to share the Gospel through the speaker box.

I spoke up and said, "Everyone, please give me your attention!" I could see people looking around the store and my friend looking out at me. I continued, "I want everyone to know tonight that God loves you and Jesus is real and He wants to give you eternal life. I am going to pray right now and, if you pray with me, you can have God's gift of eternal life."

I started praying and I could hear people asking, "Who is

that?" "Who's talking?" Just as I got my prayer out, I heard the speaker shut off. My friend returned to the car and told me that everyone had heard what I had said in the store; it was awesome.

Some may question what good that did because no one prayed with me. There is no way I could know what impact that may have had. The people in the store may have thought I was a nut job, talking about Jesus over the intercom. That's possible, but not what I believe! I believe that unless someone hears the Gospel, they will not know the Savior.

Paul wrote in Romans 10:14, *"How shall they call on Him in whom they have not believed? And how shall they believe in Him of whom they have not heard?"* He went on to say, *"How shall they hear without a preacher?"* Then Paul said in verse 17, *"So then faith comes by hearing and hearing by the word of God."*

I never second guess what the Word of God can produce and the effects that it will have on the hearer. That may seem like a ridiculous thing to do, maybe foolish to some, but Paul said, *"The foolishness of God is wiser than men, and the weakness of God is stronger than men."* He said again in 1 Corinthians 1:21, *"It pleased God through the foolishness of the message preached to save those who believe."* The bottom line is that we are God's mouthpiece and He has given us the message; it is up to us to get the message out and He will make the Word work.

10

TAKE UP YOUR CROSS

IN 1988, I attended a conference called the National Street Ministers Conference. It was the first time I had heard anyone give recognition to those who preached the Gospel on the streets. In many of the circles I traveled in, it seemed that other Christians and church leaders looked down on those who were "street preachers." There was a time that I thought the same way, and there I was at a conference for street ministry. God had turned my thinking around.

I had heard about a man who traveled the world carrying a cross. His name was Arthur Blessitt and he was one of the main speakers at this conference in Texas. After hearing his stories and the miracles that took place as he carried the cross, I decided that I, too, wanted to experience carrying the cross.

When I returned home, a friend of mine who loved working with wood built me a cross. It was ten feet tall with a six-foot cross beam. He built it out of solid, hard wood and it was heavy, just like Arthur's cross. We put a wheel on the end of the cross to keep it from dragging the ground. I was excited to start carrying the cross and to see what kind of experiences I would encounter for God.

My first time on the street with the cross was in Pueblo, Colorado on 4th Street. This was a busy street leading from where the church was located to the downtown area. The first thing I noticed as I carried the cross were the strange looks. Some would honk their horn and wave or give me a thumbs up. Others gave me hand gestures expressing their disapproval of what I was doing.

The cross has an impact on people, and even more so when you remove it from a church steeple, take it down from the wall, or are not wearing it. Carrying the cross in a public area really gets attention! In general, people are fine with Christianity, if it stays in the church building. As soon as you take Jesus to the streets, you're going to find those who approve and those who don't. I believe that if your Christianity does not grab the attention of the people, then you are "hiding it under a basket" as Jesus spoke of. Don't get me wrong, you don't have to build a cross and carry it around town, but there should be something about you that reminds people of who Jesus is.

It wasn't long before I found myself taking the cross into our downtown area on Friday and Saturday nights and standing in front of the bars, night clubs, and XXX rated porn shops. I did not do this in protest of these businesses, even though I strongly disapproved of their existence in our city. Rather, I went with the cross to speak with those who would listen about God's love for them. When you stand out in front of businesses like these, you don't have to say anything to get a response!

11

BRUNO'S BIKER BAR

I NEVER PAID much attention to bars, nightclubs, and the like. After all, I was a Christian, ordained minister, and had pastored a church, as well as served on staff at a couple of churches. I no longer lived the lifestyle that indulges in those kinds of places, yet here I was with my ten-foot cross standing about twenty feet from the door to Bruno's Biker Bar on the public sidewalk. You could not help but see me and that cross. As people would pass by me, almost every person would say some sort of negative remark. At times I thought to myself, "Why am I doing this?" Why was I subjecting myself to a bunch of negative reactions and what seemed like self-inflicted persecution?

One night, a guy came storming out of the bar with his girl-friend and he was mad as hell. I say "mad as hell" because he was full of hell's fury. He came straight toward me and I thought, *Here we go, this guy is going to unleash on me.* He got right up to my face and said, "I don't know why you think you have to stand out here and ruin everyone's night. All we are doing is trying to have a good time and you're out here screwing everything up!" His girlfriend was pulling at his arm telling him, "Honey, let's just go, he's not with it, he's just a religious fanatic." I hadn't said anything to this guy or anyone else that night. I had just stood there with the cross.

He went on to say, "What's your problem, man? What makes you think you can stand out here with a cross and bother people?" I told him in a non-confrontational, soft voice that I wasn't there to ruin his night. After my response, he asked angrily why I was there. I told him, "I am here to get your attention." He said, "Well, you've got it. What's your deal, anyway?" The door to minister had been opened. I replied, "I am here to get your attention long enough to tell you that God knows who you are, where you are, and He loves you, dude." Again, his girlfriend pulled him by the arm trying to get him to leave. I could tell that she did not want to hear anything I had to say about God. Yet this guy who came at me with such anger settled down and we began to talk.

I was not there in front of Bruno's Bar to preach a message of condemnation to sinners. John 3:17 says, *"For God did not send His Son into the world to condemn the world, but that the world through Him might be saved"* (NKJV). Too often, I have witnessed Christians condemning people in their sin rather than bringing them the Good News that will lead them out of sin.

So here we are having a conversation in front of the bar, and before the conversation was finished, the guy's girlfriend stormed off down the sidewalk and it was just the two of us. To be honest, I don't remember everything I told him that night, but I do remember praying with him to receive Jesus. Proverbs 15:1 says, *"A soft answer turns away wrath, but a harsh word stirs up anger."* The devil always wants to try and get us to respond to people in the flesh, out of our emotions, but Christ in us will respond to people by the Spirit.

12

PHONE BOOTH SALVATION

WE HAD JUST FINISHED PACKING our bus to head out on the road for a series of meetings in the Midwest. At the time, we were living in Conroe, Texas, and we had been traveling as a family for about four years, spending more and more time on the road each year. We had purchased a forty-foot MCI coach that had been converted into a custom RV for our family.

As we left town that day, we stopped by the local Walley World (Wal-Mart) to get some supplies before getting on the interstate. I parked the bus at the far end of the parking lot. Peggy and I headed across the lot to the main entrance to do our shopping. As we got closer, I heard a phone ringing. This was before we had a cell phone and when pay phones were still out in front of most stores. The closer we got to the entrance, the ringing continued and I watched people walk by the three pay phones out front ignoring the one phone that was ringing.

Like everyone else, we walked by the ringing phone, not giving it much attention. As we passed by, I heard the Holy Spirit say, "Answer the phone!" I kept walking and heard Him say again, "I said answer the phone!" I told Peggy that I would meet her inside. I turned around and went back to the phone that was ringing. By this time, the phone had been ringing for a while and when I got to the ringing phone, it suddenly stopped. I thought I had missed the call, but then it started ringing again.

Following the Holy Spirit's prompting, I picked up the phone and answered, "Hello!" A woman on the other end said, "Hi, how are you?" I replied, "I am good. What about you?" She replied by saying, "I am lonely and in need of someone to talk to. Will you talk to me?" I told her I would talk to her and asked her what she wanted to talk about. I had no clue who was on the other end. All I knew was that it was a woman and she was speaking as though she knew me personally. She had been calling and calling this number, hoping that someone would answer and talk to her. She was glad that I had answered the phone.

We exchanged names. I don't remember her name, but let's just say it was Sally for the sake of sharing this experience with you. I asked Sally if she realized that she was calling a payphone in front of Wal-Mart. She said that she did know that. I continued, "What is it that you're calling for?" Sally said, "I called just to talk with you." By this time, the Holy Spirit had revealed things to me about this woman through the word of knowledge, according to 1 Corinthians 12:8.

A word of knowledge from the Holy Spirit is knowledge about someone or something that you would not know yourself but is revealed to you by the Holy Spirit. The best example I know of is when Jesus met the woman at the well in John 4. Jesus asked the woman to go get her husband and the woman said, "I have no husband." Jesus basically replied to her, "You have spoken truly, yet you have had five husbands and are living with a man." Jesus had no knowledge of this woman or her life except what His Father was showing Him about her. She then replied to Jesus, "I perceive you're a prophet." Jesus did not say these things to condemn her, but to let her know that the Messiah, who she hoped to see one day, was standing right in front of her.

Now, back to my story. I said, "Well, Sally, you have called the right person. In fact, I have a message for you." With excitement in her voice, she replied, "What is it?" Then the Holy Spirit had me say these words, "Sally, you have been trying to find love in all the wrong places and today, once again, you're calling, hoping to meet a man to fill your need. But God is saying to you that I AM the only one who can meet your needs, I AM the one who gave His life for you, Sally. It's time for you to quit looking to men to meet your needs and look to Me, your heavenly Father, who loves you and desires to help you."

She began crying and asking me who I was and how I knew her and her situation. I told her that I didn't know who she was, but that Jesus knew and that He had told me to answer this phone and share this with her. I told her that I had no idea who would be on the other end of the line, but God did and that He wanted her to give her life to Him.

As I spoke these things, Sally was quiet. "Sally, do you hear what I am telling you? Are you ready to give your life to Jesus?" With a broken voice, she said, "Yes, I am. I don't want to live like this anymore!" I prayed with her that day over a pay phone at Wal-Mart, leading her to salvation in Jesus Christ. I gave her the name of several churches that I knew would be a good place for her to go. Then we hung up. I left that day with my heart so full of the love of God and so full of excitement and wonder at God's amazing grace.

There is no person God cannot reach. God has your number, He has my number, and the number of every person He wants to get in contact with. All He needs is someone like you and me to answer when He calls. God wants to work through us in ways that we would never think of or plan. All we need to do is obey that still small voice on the inside, step out in faith, and do the impossible!

13

COURT HOUSE ENCOUNTER

ONE NIGHT as I was driving by myself around town, I saw three guys standing outside their parked car in front of our city courthouse. I drove around the block and parked on the opposite side of the street. As I sat in my car, I asked the Lord how I could witness to these guys. I knew that I could just simply walk up to them and ask them if they knew Jesus, but I really felt I needed to use a different approach.

This was back in the early years of what I have coined as the "Holy Ghost Apprenticeship." I was learning how to hear and move as the Holy Spirit spoke and when the Holy Spirit said to go. Jesus told two brothers, Peter and Andrew, who were fishermen, in Matthew 4:19, "Follow Me, and I will make you fishers of men." These guys became Jesus' apprentices. Jesus calls them His disciples. When I first began actively and purposefully engaging people to share Christ, I asked Jesus to make me a fisher of men like He did Peter, Andrew, and His other disciples. I knew the Romans Road to Salvation and other methods of sharing the Gospel, but I wanted to be Jesus' apprentice. I had served as an apprentice with my dad learning the construction business along with several different trades. I knew what it meant to follow someone, to be at their side, to take orders, and follow instructions even when I did not totally understand why. When I would ask my dad, "Why do I need to do it this way?" his reply sometimes would be, "Because I said to!" As an apprentice, I learned that you don't always need to know why. If I followed directions and did what I was told, I usually found out why.

So, I am sitting in my car asking the Lord how to reach these three guys. The thought came to me, run across the street hollering, "Hey, did you guys hear the good news?" As you might imagine, I thought that sounded a little nutty! If I go running up to these three guys like that, they are liable to either run off or beat me with a stick.

Have you ever had the Lord ask you to pray for the person in front of you in the checkout at the store or have you ask that person if you can pray for them? When that happens, your heart begins to feel like it's somehow up in your throat, your mouth dries up instantly, and you start to sweat profusely. Do you know what I am talking about? This is exactly how I was feeling, sitting in my car, looking across the street at these three guys just hanging out.

Pushing my feelings and reservations aside, I decide to give it a shot! I got out of my car and burst across the street, running at full speed hollering, "Hey, did you hear?" These guys were startled to say the least. "Hear what?" I said, "The good news!" They replied, "What good news?" As I approached, I slowed down and stopped just a few feet from them to catch my breath. Of course, they were curious and wanted to know what I was talking about. I continued, "You haven't heard the good news yet?" They all looked at each other with a surprised, confused look and said, "Guess not, what 'good news'?" I said, "God sent me here to find you because He wants you guys to give your hearts to Jesus."

Immediate laughing came from all three. "Dude, what are

you talking about? Is this a joke?" I told them that I was serious, and that God sent me there to talk to them about giving their lives to Jesus. I explained to them that God has a plan for their lives and that He wants to give them salvation, forgiveness of sin, and real purpose. By this time, they knew that I was serious. I could feel the presence of God and the anointing flowing through my words. I felt as though Jesus Himself was speaking through my lips. The truth is, when we yield to the Holy Spirit and His power, He does speak through us when we become that yielded vessel. Jesus said, *"For I will give you a mouth and wisdom, which all your adversaries shall not be able to gainsay nor resist"* (Luke 21:15 KJV).

I watched as the anointing of God came upon these three guys. I could feel the love of God saturating the atmosphere. I asked them, "You know that God is here, right?" All three nodded in agreement. I told them, "He is talking to your hearts, am I right?" All three nodded yes. I asked them if I could pray with all three of them, to receive Jesus as Lord and ask Him to show them His plan for their lives. They all agreed. I pulled my little leather-bound New Testament Bible out of my back pocket and turned quickly to Romans 10:9-13. I had these Scriptures underlined in my Bible. I explained to them what God's Word says about confessing with your mouth and believing with your heart. I asked, "Do you guys believe God is real?" All three replied with a resounding, "Yes!" I asked, "Do you believe He loves you and sent Jesus to be your Savior and Lord?" Again, they replied, "Yes." "Will you confess with me tonight with your own mouth that Jesus is your Lord?" They said, "Yes!" Each one confessed with me that Jesus is Lord and thanked Him for saving them and giving them eternal life. They were so ready and willing. Praise God!

Can it really be that easy? Is it possible that they were just agreeing with me to get rid of me? These thoughts are not God's thoughts; they are thoughts of unbelief. The devil tries to change our faith to doubt. His goal is for us to doubt God and His Word, and ultimately to doubt ourselves when we obey God's word. Second Corinthians 4:6 says this: *"For it is God who commanded light to shine out of darkness, who has shone in our hearts to give the light of the knowledge of the glory of God in the face of Jesus Christ"* (NKJV). The Holy Spirit is the one that takes our witness and uses it to convince others of their need for Christ. God's Word brings light and that light reveals a person's need for Jesus. I love Psalm 119:130: *"The entrance of Your words gives light; It gives understanding to the simple."*

Never underestimate what God can do through a believer who will yield themselves to be used by the Holy Spirit. It is awesome!

14

KNOCK, KNOCK?

AFTER RECEIVING my ministry ordination in 1984, Peggy and I moved to the small town of Penrose, Colorado to start a Bible study and outreach. During the week, I would knock on doors and talk to people about the Lord. My mother-in-law, Pauline, would accompany me on these outings to keep things above reproach. As a young married man knocking on doors, the doors would often be opened by a young mother caring for the children and/or a wife caring for the home while her husband was at work. I made sure to have someone with me as not to give the devil any opportunity. It also made it possible for us to go inside the home to visit and minister to a person if invited to do so. Mark 6:7 says, *"And he called unto him the twelve, and began to send them forth by two and two; and gave them power over unclean spirits."*

I found myself knocking on a door alone one day. I don't remember exactly why I was alone, but I remember that I purposed in my heart that if invited in I would simply decline the invitation and offer to come back another day. I drove down a dirt road out in the country and pulled into a gravel driveway. From appearances, it looked as though someone was at home.

A car was in the driveway and the curtains in the front of the house were opened. As I walked up the steps of the front porch, I could see an elderly lady sitting in a chair watching TV. My first thoughts were that I was glad someone was at home and that this lady looked like a nice, old grandma.

I knocked on the door a couple of times before she got up to answer. She opened the door rather abruptly and, before I could say anything, she said, "Yes, what do you want?" Immediately, I found myself apologizing to her in hopes that I had not disturbed her. I asked, "Yes, ma'am, I hope I am not disturbing you?" She said, "Well, it's too late for that." I apologized again. She responded quickly with, "What do you want?" I told her that I was visiting people in our community, gave her my name and explained I was a minister, and asked her if I could pray with her. The woman abruptly replied, "No!"

I went on to ask her if I could ask some questions and she was definitely not interested in hearing anything I had to say. Her response was, "I don't have time for this right now. I have a migraine headache and I need to go sit back down." I told her, "Hey, let me pray for you, lay hands on your head, and believe Jesus to heal you of this headache." All of a sudden, she pulled the door wide open and said, "Get in here!"

Wow. Glory to God, this grandma is going to let me pray for her and God is going to heal her. She did not ask me or invite me to sit down. She commanded that I sit down. So I did. She walked over to a table, picked up a book, and then sat down across from me. It was a Bible. She asked me where my Bible was. I pulled out my little New Testament and showed her. She further inquired, "Where is the rest of your Bible? That's just the New Testament, right?"

Before I knew what was happening, she started hurling Scriptures at me from the Old Testament and asking me questions left and right. Within just a few minutes, I felt like a whipped pup and just wanted to get out of this woman's house!

She asked me questions about things that I did not have answers for. I do remember feeling overwhelmed as confusion filled the room. I knew that something was not right. I did not know what this woman believed; however, I did know what she believed was not the same as what I believed. Every time I tried to give an answer, she just hammered me with another Scripture that didn't fit or make sense.

I asked her several times to explain the point she was making. Her reply was, "You don't know your Bible and you came here to talk to me? You want to pray for me when you can't understand the Bible for yourself!" Her words were like arrows hurling through the air. I wondered what I had gotten myself into. Thoughts of insecurity filled my mind. I asked the Lord what to say. "Holy Spirit, help me" was my plea. Immediately prompted by the Holy Spirit, I opened my mouth and said, "What do you believe about the baptism of the Holy Spirit? And speaking in tongues?" She stopped talking and looked at me like I had hit her in the head with a hammer.

I took the moment to tell her that God wanted to give her eternal life and to fill her with the Holy Ghost. She told me that the Holy Spirit and speaking in tongues was not for today. She said that this was something only the apostles had. I told her that any person who believes can receive. "Watch this!" I exclaimed. I began speaking in other tongues. She stood up from her chair and moved toward the door. "Young man, it's time for you to leave."

By this time, I was more than glad to get out of there. I stepped out of her house and onto the porch; she slammed the door. I remember feeling as though I had been beat up and thrown out. My mind was thinking that I blew it and that I didn't even know how to witness to an old lady. Those thoughts were not from God. The devil is the one who brings condemnation, not God!

"There is no condemnation now for those who live in union
with Christ Jesus." (Romans 8:1 GNB)

As I walked toward my car feeling like a failure, I heard the
woman's voice call out, "Young man, young man!" I wanted to
ignore her, but didn't. I turned, looked back, and replied, "Yes,
ma'am?" She told me to come back to the house. She had something she needed to tell me. My immediate thought was, *Oh
God, no. I have had enough of this woman already*. I hesitated for a
moment, but decided to return.

As I approached the porch, she stepped out from the
doorway and onto the porch. With resolution, she said, "I am a
Mormon and have been for over 30 years. I want you to know,
young man, that you have not changed me today." I thought,
That is for sure. Then she said with a bit calmer voice, "I see
something about you that makes me want to reevaluate what I
believe! Thank you for coming by." And with that, she went
inside, closing the door behind her. I got in my car, and as I
drove away, the Holy Spirit said, "Good job, son, she has a lot to
think about!" In Mark 4:14, Jesus said, *"The sower sows the word."*

15

GOT DIRECTIONS TO HEAVEN?

IT WAS ABOUT 3:00 in the afternoon. I was sitting at my desk at the church. I had just finished some paperwork when the church secretary came by my office and asked if I would be willing to take some important papers to the Post Office and stop by the office supply store to pick up some items she had ordered. My answer was yes, as I looked for any reason to get out of the office and outside the four walls of the church building.

As an evangelist and the person responsible for the outreach ministry at the church, my desire was to go where the sinners were. I wanted to be around people who needed Jesus; not just counsel Christians, who many times were just too lazy to get into the Word for themselves. Peggy and I spent three years pastoring and we had our share of counseling with church people, who for the most part, just wanted to air their grievances and get you to agree with their viewpoint. Enough about that subject!

I gathered up the stuff that needed to go to the Post Office, grabbed a check from the secretary to pay for the supplies, and out the door I went. I made my stop by the Post Office and then on to the office supply store. Because this store was just off of the main street, which happened to be a one-way street, I drove around looking for a place to park. I was stopped at the traffic light preparing to turn right. I noticed several people on the right waiting to cross the street; however, they seemed to be too busy talking to each other and not paying attention to the light.

My passenger side window was down. The Holy Spirit prompted me to ask the people for directions. Wait, wasn't I looking for a place to park? And now I'm asking for directions? I knew where I was going! I decided to ask them for directions, directions on how to get to heaven. I leaned over toward the passenger side door and hollered to the group standing on the corner, "Hey, can you give me some directions?" This guy broke away from the group, told me yes, and then told me to pull around the corner.

I made a right turn and pulled over, kind of double parked, and a couple guys came to my side of the car and asked me what I was looking for. I replied, "I need directions to heaven." The one guy looked at the other and said, "Do you know of any street named heaven?" The other guy said, "Nope." You couldn't script this. Seeing that they didn't understand what I was asking, I said, "You must have misunderstood me. I am not looking for a street, but directions on how to get to heaven." Both of them looked at each other and started laughing. One responded, "Are you talking about heaven, as in God and angels and all that kind of stuff?" I said, "Yeah, do you know how to get there?" Again, they both started laughing and one of them said, "No, serious man, where are you wanting to get to?" I said, "I told you, heaven!" Then the other guy chimed in and said, with a little frustration, "I think you're asking the wrong people here. Maybe you need to go to a church somewhere."

I started to laugh and told them, "No, I am just messing with you!" They seemed relieved and ready to move on, so I asked them for a quick minute. "If you guys don't know how to get to heaven, I just happen to have the direction right here." Both of them replied, "No way! Are you serious?" I whipped out my New Testament and took them to John 14:6 NKJV: *"Jesus said, 'I am the way, the truth, and the life. No one comes to the Father except through Me.'"* I explained to them that they were right about God being in heaven and the angels, but the only way they would ever get to heaven is by calling on the name of Jesus as their Lord.

As soon as those words left my mouth, I could sense the anointing of God right there. The Holy Spirit was right in our midst. His power was convincing these guys that what I was saying was true. The power of God, His anointing in us, is released when we speak the Gospel message. As ridiculous as my approach seemed, the Holy Spirit used it to reach both of these men. That day, while doubled parked in the middle of the road, I asked these guys if they wanted to receive Jesus in their hearts and know that they have eternal life. Their response was YES! Praise God, it was awesome! In a matter of a few minutes —time's totally off the cuff—the Holy Spirit gave me a creative way to reach out to a couple of people who had no idea God had set them up for a divine appointment with Jesus that day.

16

TOILETS & TRACTS

THE FIRST YEAR or so working with the church, I tried all kinds of ways to get people from outside to come in, to win the lost. We tried pizza parties with the youth, we tried having concerts with Christian bands in the parking lot, and many more Christian events trying to reach lost people. Out of frustration one day, I told the Lord, "The people in this city don't want God! There are churches on nearly every corner and 24-hour Christian broadcasting on TV. If people want You, God, they can come and find You."

You can pretty much guess that I was about to receive some instructions from the Lord. He replied back to me and said, "When did you ever see fish come jump in a boat to go for a ride? Fish don't ride in boats, they don't swim on dry ground, and they don't come to church. If you want fish, you have to go do what it takes to catch them!" I started thinking about that and the things Jesus said about following Him and becoming fishers of men.

God went on to tell me, "Tim, you were not born again as a fisherman. You can read about fishing, you can buy all kinds of fishing gear, and talk about how you're going to fish, but until you get out where the fish are and cast your line, you're not going to have much success." The Lord began showing me how I had expected lost people to come to church, come to our evangelism Christian events, and how most lost people have no interest in going to church. The Holy Spirit said to me, "Tim, if you will lead them to Christ, they will have a reason to come to church." Believe it or not, that was a real revelation to me at the time. I also realized that the world has all kinds of events that pay big money to put on and all I have to do is show up!

I heard about one of these events that would be taking place in a few weeks. It was a street concert put on by Budweiser Beer. I saw flyers posted and heard radio spots broadcasted for this event coming to town. I got with several of my friends who had been going out on the streets of Pueblo with me and told them that we needed to get to this event and pass out tracts. I even told them that maybe we would get on stage and preach to thousands of people at the event. We all got excited about this adventure and spent time preparing.

Then the time had come for the big event. We gathered at the church to pray for about thirty minutes before hitting the streets and then we headed to Main Street. You could hear the bands getting ready to rock the place. Excitement was growing in us all as we parked the car and began walking a couple blocks to the concert. To our surprise, it looked huge; there were people everywhere drinking beer and getting into the music. What we had not considered was that this was a rock concert... Duh! You could not hear yourself think, let alone talk to anyone about Jesus.

For the next hour or so, we walked through the crowd hoping for some kind of miraculous opportunity to arise. I imagined myself somehow getting up on the stage with all the lights and someone handing me a mic, then preaching Christ and the power of God hitting that place! That did not happen.

After a couple hours of hanging around, we all decided that we would call it a night.

As we were walking down the street, we passed the side street where we had parked to head to some porta-johns (portable toilets or PJ as I will call them) to take care of business before heading back to the church. As I stood in line waiting, I looked around to see that there were dozens of these toilets on each side of the street and they all had people standing in line waiting for a turn. I believe it was the Holy Spirit that gave me the idea to put a gospel tract inside these PJs.

When I went in and after I was finished, I closed the lid and laid a tract on top of the toilet seat lid. Then I got back in line to go see if the tract got thrown down or dumped in the toilet. To my surprise and delight, I watched this person come out of the PJ putting the bright yellow tract in his shirt pocket. After seeing the first response to the tract, I told the other guys with me, "Hey, I just left a tract in the PJ and some guy picked it up and put it in his pocket!" We all spent the next hour or so going from toilet to toilet putting tracts on the seats and watching people put them in their pockets! It was awesome! We must have passed out several hundred tracts that night putting the Gospel in the hands of people. Who knows what effect it had, but I learned that night that God will make a way if you are willing to follow!

17

RIGHT HEART, WRONG IDEA

BACK IN THE early days of my Holy Ghost apprenticeship, ministering on the streets, there were times when I had a good idea, but not a God idea, if you know what I mean. One night, a friend by the name of Vince and I were downtown looking for opportunities to share Christ with people. That particular night, for whatever reason, no one was hanging out. It seemed like everyone was just cruising around Main Street in their cars with their music thumping away. It was a little chilly that night, but that usually did not stop people from standing outside of their cars. We tried and tried to get someone to pull over so we could witness to them.

Finally, I came up with this idea to get Vince to lie down on the sidewalk and pretend to be hurt. I would give him chest compressions as if he were having some kind of heart attack. Vince was an ex-gang member who was usually up for anything and not afraid to try new things. When the last group of cars passed us and there was a break in the flow of traffic, Vince laid down on the cold hard sidewalk. I told Vince to close his eyes and not to smile; we were always making each other laugh. I told him, "Lay still and when the next group of cars come up to the stop light, I will start giving you CPR!"

The next group of cars stopped when the light turned red, so I started doing chest compressions (lightly) and people began to holler out of their windows. "Hey, you need someone to call an ambulance?" "Is that guy all right?" "What happened?" Cars began to pull over and people started coming over to see what had happened. I told Vince again to lie still and not to move. The plan was to jump up and start preaching to them when a large crowd had gathered.

Clearly, this was a bad idea. You might even be thinking right now, *What in God's name were you guys thinking, doing something so stupid?* I know, I was there! Anyway, just about the time I was going to tell Vince to jump up, we heard the sirens; the fire and rescue showed up. I told Vince that we needed to get out of there. We both jumped up to everyone's surprise and I hollered, "He is healed, he is healed!" A guy standing right behind me said, "Wait, the ambulance is on its way; let them check this guy out!" I told the man that Vince was fine. We ran to my car, jumped in, and took off down an alley. We made a few turns here and there, and then headed back to the church. We both felt really stupid. In fact, what we did bothered me for a long time. Thank God no one got hurt and we weren't responsible for an accident.

I hesitated to share this story, simply because, to this day, I am ashamed of pulling such a dumb stunt. However, I do share this because it just proves that not every idea is inspired by God. Sometimes we can do things that we think are good ideas when in reality it's not. God never condemned me over that mistake, but He did ask me if I learned anything. There is a difference between the Holy Spirit leading you and you leading you. It's easy to let our own ideas get in the way. This experience did not hinder me from stepping out from that day on, but it did cause me to think twice as to whether or not I was doing something out of a zeal for God, or if it was the Holy Spirit actually leading me. I want to encourage anyone reading this, that you're going to make mistakes in life and ministry, and that's ok as long as you let the Holy Spirit teach you. Don't let the devil condemn you over a mistake. God is bigger than any mistake we can ever make. Just keep your heart right and stay teachable and you will succeed!

18

TRACT & TREAT

BACK IN THE MID 1980S, many churches were realizing the need to provide an alternative for children in place of Halloween and the whole "trick or treat" experience. When I was growing up as a kid in the '60s, most people knew their neighbors and they could be trusted. You could send your children out into the neighborhood and never give it a second thought. By the 1980s, our culture in many places around the United States had changed. There were more and more reports of child abduction, candy laced with drugs or poison, and the fear of the occult. By 1987, I was ministering a lot on the streets of our city and looking for different ways to help the church reach out. By that time, our home church was doing what they called a Hallelujah Party in place of either having a costume party and candy or just not participating at all and leaving families to do whatever. Even though the church was hosting a Hallelujah Party, I was looking for a more aggressive approach to reaching the unchurched people in our community.

The Holy Spirit gave me an idea and I call it "Tract & Treat." We knew a lady who was a talented artist, as well as a pastor with her husband. To this day, thirty years later, we still preach for them and their church. I had an idea for a Gospel tract that would have a picture of Jesus standing at a door knocking. Sound familiar? *"Behold, I stand at the door and knock. If anyone hears My voice and opens the door, I will come in to him and dine with him, and he with Me"* (Revelation 3:20 NKJV). The picture would have children and their parents on the other side of the door answering... you get the picture. Our friend, Dianna, made a sketch of what I was seeing in my mind and did a great job.

We took her sketch, added some Scripture, and took it to print. I was so excited to get these tracts! I still use them to this day. The Holy Spirit told me to get small white paper bags (lunch bags) and put some other Gospel materials in the bag: mini book on salvation, Gospel of John, and something about our church inviting them to come and get some candy. Then I took the tract and stapled it to the top of the bag. I could not wait for Halloween to roll around!

I remember taking these bags with tracts and Gospel treats and going door to door on Halloween night, knocking on the door or ringing the doorbell from house to house. There were so many surprised expressions on people's faces when they saw that it wasn't a bunch of children but rather a guy with an arm load of bags. People would say things like, "Who are you supposed to be? Aren't you a little old to be doing this? Where is your costume?" I received all different kinds of responses. My response was the same, "I am not here to get a treat, but to give you one and without any tricks!" As far as I remember, no one rejected my Gospel bags.

One year when we lived in Texas, we decided to get a number of people from the congregation to go with us door to door on Halloween night to distribute our Tract & Treat bags. We went out in the area neighborhoods of Humble, Texas, where the church was located. Some of the people from the church were a little unsure of going door to door, but I assured them that if there was any time of the year that people are receptive to someone knocking on their door, it was Halloween. People would leave their porch light on as a way of saying that a knock was welcome. If the light was off and the curtains were drawn shut, we just moved on to the next house.

We arrived in the first neighborhood and unloaded our cars. I instructed everyone to go in pairs. The plan was to meet back in about twenty minutes. As I started out, I noticed how many of the parents were out with their children going house to house. I realized quickly that not only did we have an opportunity to reach those living in the homes we were going to, but also the parents of the children gathered out on the sidewalk in front of the houses waiting for their kids to get their treats. I never tried giving children these bags without asking the parents first. A parent didn't want some stranger approaching their child with a goody bag; some things are just common sense. We would give the parents a bag first as they were waiting for their child, then make our way to the door to hand out the Tract & Treat bags to the homeowner.

Time and time again, those answering the door would say, "That's a first," as we handed the bags to them and then thank us for the gift. I would ask the people at the door if I could pray with them about anything. Most of the time, the people would reply that all was good. From time to time, others would ask if I was from a church, and, if so, what church I was from. Occasionally, there would be a person who did not like the idea we were out spreading the Gospel on a night that actually has been used to magnify the devil. Regardless of the response, we were ready with an answer from the Holy Ghost. Over the years as I have taken people out from different churches, they have witnessed how open people are to the Gospel. We would pray with parents to receive Jesus as they waited for their kids.

All it takes is one God-inspired idea acted upon to change lives for eternity! God is not confused nor is He puzzled about how to reach a generation of people. Regardless of how culture changes, where people live, what country they are from, God has a way for you and me to reach them with the greatest message mankind will ever hear.

Romans 10:14-15 says, *"How then shall they call on Him in whom they have not believed? And how shall they believe in Him of whom they have not heard? And how shall they hear without a preacher? And how shall they preach unless they are sent? As it is written: 'How beautiful are the feet of those who preach the gospel of peace, Who bring glad tidings of good things'"* (NKJV).

19

WORK AND THE MINISTRY

DURING THE YEARS I attended Bible school, and up until 1994, I worked construction on the side. In 1984, when Peggy and I started our outreach ministry, Living Word Outreach, our desire and purpose was to reach "unchurched" people with the Gospel. We wanted to reach those who were stuck in religion and unaware of the goodness of God and the power of the Holy Spirit available to them. During those first few years of ministry, I worked construction with my dad and started my own business. I ran my own business from 1989-1994 until we relocated to Texas. During this first decade of our ministry, even though it may have seemed as though we weren't very successful from the outside, God was building us from the inside out.

The first three years of ministry, we had people gathering weekly; this gathering was basically a church grown out of our outreach in the community. While we never grew very large in numbers, God used this time to train me on how to communicate better with people and gave me insight into what it was to pastor a church—the good, the bad, and the ugly. As the saying goes, "The grass always looks greener on the other side of the fence." I have known many pastors over the years who thought that the traveling ministry looked like a vacation compared to what they had to deal with, and the same holds true for those traveling in ministry who thought that pastoring a church would be a better gig. The truth is that you will only be successful when you find, follow, and fulfill the call that God has given you specifically.

There is a special grace given to each of us to do what God has called us to do. Paul instructs us in Romans 12:3 saying, *"For I say, through the grace given to me, to everyone who is among you, not to think of himself more highly than he ought to think, but to think soberly, as God has dealt to each one a measure of faith."* Think about that. Paul did what he did, and said what he said, not based on his ability or his desires, but through the grace given to him. Grace is God's ability to work in and through us to do what we cannot do ourselves.

We are not just saved by grace through faith; everything we do for Christ and the ministry He has called us to is according to the grace given to us. Saving grace is the same, but then there is God's equipping grace. Look at this statement Paul makes in Ephesians 3:7 (NKJV): *"...of which I became a minister according to the gift of the grace of God given to me by the effective working of His power."* It always does you good to go back and look at the context in which something is being said; you will find that what I am saying about the equipping grace from God is true.

During those first years in ministry, we did not have a worldwide well-known ministry. In fact, I felt, at times, that God may have overlooked me and forgot that He called me into ministry! It was certain that men, even other ministers, did not always consider me a person who was "in the ministry." I am sharing these things because if I had listened to those who looked at me and even, at times, treated me as less than a "minister of the Gospel," called by God as an evangelist, I would have eventually given up and would not be where God has brought me to today.

In the Christian church circles that we were associated with and working with, most people, including pastors, did not consider a person as a real minister until that person was in "full-time ministry." Which means that the person didn't work in a secular job. To be considered "full-time ministry," a person had to be living from the money that the ministry provided. This wasn't the case for me. For a number of years, as God was building the ministry He called us to and building us with a strong foundation, I worked 40-60 hours a week and even worked seasonal part-time work. I did more ministry out in the highways and byways leading people to Jesus and experiencing God's miracle working power during those times than any other time in my life! Since 1994, I have not worked a permanent secular job. From time to time, I have done things or worked to make extra money on the side if time allowed. The majority of my time has been spent working in the ministry and traveling full-time.

We have been to 33 countries around the world ministering, traveling to churches across the United States month after month and year after year. We have conducted local, city-wide, and national outreach events leading thousands to Christ over the past 25 years. Our ministry has responded to tens of thousands during natural disasters, including the most recent in 2018, Hurricane Michael in Florida. God has used my natural abilities, talents, and my trade experience to build a number of tiny houses in the garbage dumps of Mexico and churches from the ground up. I've had building projects in Romania, India, and the United States. What I learned working, not only before I went into the ministry, but especially the few years following, God has used to make me a fisher of men on the job site. God has taught me through those years of working construction and ministry how to plan ahead, how to organize, and how to work with different types of people and backgrounds.

Today, we lead hundreds of people in outreaches and we plan and organize events that touch thousands with the Gospel. We have to be ready to leave within hours to respond to a disaster, organizing semi loads of goods to help, mobilizing groups of volunteers whom we may not know or have worked with, and more. We work with people of different church backgrounds, and even different religions, and maintain a good witness for Christ, all the while being productive and completing the tasks at hand. All of this God had planned and was working in us during those years that we didn't seem to be seeing many results. We didn't look like "full-time ministry" in comparison to others who seemed to be receiving the recognition and acknowledgment.

We are celebrating 36 years of ministry! I thank Jesus for all of those years of what did not look like much, but where He was building us from the inside out. We have watched many over the years shipwreck, we have seen many marriages fail in the ministry, and we have witnessed families destroyed. There is nothing that God cannot heal, restore, and bring back to life. It is far better to follow Jesus step by step, let Him build you into the man or woman of God He desires for you to be, and bring you into the ministry that only He has the grace to give you to succeed.

Ministry is spelled W-O-R-K, whether preaching behind a pulpit or on the streets, sharing Jesus with someone at work or school, a neighbor, a family member, or a complete stranger. No matter the situation or circumstance, ministry is work. God is looking for those who will take up their cross and follow Him to work. Paul instructs us in Ephesians 4:11-12 that we are to be equipped for the *"work of ministry."* Jesus said to His disciples, *"The harvest is truly plentiful, but the laborers are few"* (Matthew 9:37). Jesus instructs His disciples to pray the Lord of the harvest to send laborers out into the field. Jesus calls the ministry a work of labor! You may not be called by God to be a Pastor, Evangelist, Teacher, Apostle, or Prophet, but every believer is called by Jesus to be His witness and His Gospel messenger and to labor in His harvest.

The best place to minister is right where you are!

20

TELL IT FROM THE HOUSETOP!

I WILL NEVER FORGET READING this Scripture in Matthew 10:27 NLT: "*What I tell you now in the darkness, shout abroad when daybreak comes. What I whisper in your ear, shout from the house-tops for all to hear!*" I made a decision early in my Christian walk, especially after I received the baptism of the Holy Spirit and spoke in other tongues, that whenever and wherever the Holy Spirit asked me to preach, I would. Within a few years, I had preached about Jesus to people on the streets, in front of bars and nightclubs, in hospitals and nursing care facilities, in jails and prisons, as well as on the job to those I worked with. The day I read this verse, I realized that I had never shouted the Good News from a housetop.

On one particular day, I was on a scaffolding about thirty feet in the air. I had been laying brick on a fireplace chimney. As I finished laying the last brick, I decided that I was going to stand on the peak of the roof—not the scaffolding but the roof —and preach to all the workers on the ground. I was going to shout the Gospel from the housetop! We were working in a housing development and there were contractors and laborers everywhere. From plumbers to carpenters to electricians to drywallers and more, there were a lot of people in the housing development working. It was a hopping place with lots of activity!

As noon approached, I worked as fast as I could to get the chimney done so I could get out of the Texas heat and off of the shaky scaffolding. Ten 'til noon, I laid the last brick and began cleaning up my work. When noon time came, it got a lot quieter as equipment shut down, the sound of saws stopped, and the guys found a shady place to sit and eat their lunch. As planned, I stepped onto the very steep roof peak. It was what I considered to be a big Texas roof! Holding on to the side of the chimney, careful not to dislodge any of my freshly laid brick, I hollered out with a loud voice, "Everyone, give me your attention please!" Guys began looking around and looking up toward the sound of my voice.

When I saw that I had the attention of about a dozen workers, I said, "Today is a special day! Today is the day that the Lord has made. He wants you to know He loves you and that today is your day to get saved." To be honest, some of these guys probably thought I was nuts and had been in the sun too long. Others just shook their heads and went back to eating their lunch as I continued to share for two or three minutes a word of salvation through Jesus Christ. I said, "I want everyone to know that Jesus said there is only one way to God and it's not church and it's not religion, but it is through believing in and calling on the name of Jesus Christ. Jesus said, 'I am the way, not a way, I am the truth and I am the life.'" After shouting it from the housetop, I climbed down and found a shady place to eat my lunch. Nobody said anything to me, except one of our laborers who said, "You're a crazy man!" My reply was, "Crazy for Jesus!"

I don't know that preaching from that housetop did anything for anyone on the ground that day, but it did something for me. I realized that the devil had no say in where or when I preached the Gospel and who I preached the Gospel to. I didn't have to be intimidated and I didn't have to be scared to preach to anyone, even co-workers. If the devil does try to intimidate me, I can laugh in his face and say, "Devil, do you remember when I stood on the housetop and proclaimed God to everyone on the ground? I was not ashamed then and I am not ashamed now. In Jesus' name, get thee behind me!" Romans 1:16 says, *"For I am not ashamed of the gospel of Christ, for it is the power of God to salvation for everyone who believes, for the Jew first and also for the Greek"* (NKJV). *"Therefore do not be ashamed of the testimony of our Lord, nor of me His prisoner, but share with me in the sufferings for the gospel according to the power of God"* (2 Timothy 1:8 NKJV). Words to live by.

21

A MAN, A MISSION, A MISTAKE

AFTER MERGING two churches in 1987, I worked a secular job for a five-month period. I went to work for a company laying block for a new jail complex being built in Canon City, Colorado, before taking a position at a church as Evangelist on staff later that year.

During that year, I had a strong desire to go out of the country and preach the Gospel overseas. God had brought a special person into my life, Missionary Evangelist Burnie Davis. Burnie was in his early 50s and well known. He had spent many years preaching large miracle crusades with amazing results. Burnie and his wife Dolly moved from Houston, Texas, to Colorado in the mid-'80s, and I had the opportunity to meet him, spend a lot of time with him, and later started traveling with him on a few occasions.

Burnie invited me to go with him in the spring of 1987 to India for a large miracle crusade with thousands in attendance. I had heard many of Burnie's stories and testimonies and wanted desperately to go with him. He said, "Tim, if you come, I will have you preach, and pray for the sick; you will see God do miracles." I started telling people I was going to India with

Burnie. I prayed and asked God to make a way, as it was going to cost over $4,000 for me to go. At that time, I had just started working construction. I had been on the job two weeks and decided to speak with the job foreman about getting ten days off to go to India. I was hesitant to do so, because I did not want to lose this job. Peggy and I were experiencing financial difficulties, because there was not a lot of work available. The church we were pastoring barely had enough to pay its expenses, let alone a salary for us. Even though I knew there was a chance the foreman would be angry, I decided to ask for the time off anyway.

It was a Monday morning I will never forget. I showed up early to talk to the foreman. I told him that I appreciated the job and wanted to continue to work as long as they needed me, but I had a favor to ask. His first response was that he wasn't giving any raises at this time. I told him I wasn't there for a raise. He said, "Good," and proceeded to tell me that they weren't putting any more money out on this job because the job was over budget and behind schedule. I got straight to the point and told him that I needed to have two weeks off. Before I could tell him why, he barked at me, "I just told you we are behind schedule on this project and I need you on the job or I will replace you. I have a waiting list of guys ready to work." I told him okay and that I understood. I told him I was here to work.

As I walked toward the door, my mind was swimming with thoughts: stay and work, or go to India with Burnie and lose my job? As I opened the door of the little office trailer, John said, "Wait a minute. What in the **** did you want two weeks off for?" I told him. "I believe God wants me to go to India to preach in a crusade." What did I have to lose by sharing this information? John knew I was a Christian and a preacher. He may just fire me anyway. When I was hired, John made it clear to me that he was not a believer and he did not want me preaching to everyone on the job site. John said, "You want to go to India? To preach?" I said, "Yes, sir!" And he continues, "And you think God wants you to go?" And I replied again, "Yes, sir, I believe He does." John says, "I tell you what, Preacher, who am I to go against God? Go ahead and plan your trip." Of course, I had to know, "Will I have a job when I get back?" He said, "Yes, I will keep your spot open. Now get out of here and go to work!"

I was so blessed that I got the time off and still kept my job! The next hurdle was going to get enough money to go to India as we were barely making it and I was running behind on my bills. I told God that I was believing He would supply me with the $4,000 I needed for the trip and extra to take care of things while I was gone.

I am about to share an important lesson that I learned the hard way! I don't suggest that anyone should learn through the S.O.H.K., "School of Hard Knocks." That is one of the reasons why today our ministry has S.O.M.E., *School of Mission Evangelism*. There is no reason for anyone to learn by their mistakes if they are willing to learn by the Word of God and submit to others who have the life experience of years of ministry under their belts. God gave us many examples in His Word so that we can learn what and what not to do! Read what the Apostle Paul wrote in 1 Corinthians 10:11-12 NKJV: *"Now all these things happened to them as examples, and they were written for our admonition, upon whom the ends of the ages have come. Therefore let him who thinks he stands take heed lest he fall."* It would benefit you to go read this chapter in context, but Paul was sharing mistakes and disobedience of others for our benefit so that we can learn from their mistakes and not repeat them.

Back to my story. First of all, I was believing God to supply me with what was a large amount of money in a rather short period of time—not that God could not do that, because He can! The problem I did not recognize was that I had really never went to the Lord to ask Him. I never asked, "God, do You want me to go to India with Burnie? Do You want me to go on this trip coming up in a few months?" See, I had the desire, I had the invitation, and I even had the time off from work; it all looked like it was a go and I was excited!

As the weeks passed and time grew closer and closer, absolutely no money had come in to cover the cost. I had to have a deposit in to cover the price of the airfare ticket and it looked like it was not going to happen. I kept asking the Lord, "Lord, where is the money? You know I am believing You to supply all my needs." The time finally arrived when I had to pay for the ticket and I just did not have the money. I told Burnie that I couldn't understand. I explained to him that everything seemed to come together, with the exception of the funds needed to make the trip. Long story short, I had to cancel my plans, tell everyone at church that I was not going after all, and then go to my boss and tell him I was not going. It was a hard pill to swallow and I was pretty disappointed!

As I was driving home from work one day, I told God that I didn't understand. What did I do wrong? I was smart enough not to blame God for my financial shortfall, but I was thinking I just did not have enough faith to believe Him for it. The Lord spoke to me and said, "Son, what did I tell you to do in My Word?" I immediately recalled the words of Jesus and how He said to them, *"Go ye into all the world and preach the gospel to every creature."* Then the Lord said, "That's right, but where did I tell you to start?" Jesus told His disciples in Acts 1:8, *"But you shall receive power when the Holy Spirit has come upon you; and you shall be witnesses to Me in Jerusalem, and in all Judea and Samaria, and to the end of the earth."*

The Lord said, "Son, you want to go to India and preach, but you're not going to your own city, to your own people, speaking your own language, and telling them about Me." I knew the Lord was right. Going to some far-off place overseas seemed much more exciting and much more important than saying, "I go and preach to people in Pueblo, Colorado."

From that moment on, I understood why I did not get to go to India on that trip with my friend and mentor Burnie Davis. First, I never really went to the Lord and asked Him about going before I said I was going and planned to go. Second, I used poor planning and made assumptions rather than moving out of a place of real faith. Had I inquired of the Lord with an open heart, I would have saved myself the disappointment and the embarrassment of telling people that I was going to do something for the Lord and then not doing it. Also, more importantly is the fact that I did not put God first in my plans. Read these verses, keeping what I have shared in mind.

> "Come now, you who say, 'Today or tomorrow we will go to such and such a city, spend a year there, buy and sell, and make a profit'; whereas you do not know what will happen tomorrow. For what is your life? It is even a vapor that appears for a little time and then vanishes away. Instead you ought to say, 'If the Lord wills, we shall live and do this or that.' But now you boast in your arrogance. All such boasting is evil." (James 4:13-16, NKJV)

The bottom line is that God wants to be first in our lives. While there is nothing wrong with making plans, we do need to seek first His kingdom and His righteousness. I have learned over the years that not every good idea I have about doing things for God is what He is telling me to do. Even this book you're reading right now is not the result of doing what I want or feel I need to, as we have many pressing things that need attention in our ministry at this time; but doing what God has instructed me to do. I inquired of the Lord, "Lord, what do You want me to do coming into 2019? Is there anything I need to change or do different?" He said it was time for me to write my first book. He said, "I want you to clear your schedule and get it done!" It is hard for me to sit still. I am always on the go and I enjoy being busy, and I am productive. To sit down for hours and days at a time and write seemed almost too hard to me. Yet, as I obeyed the instruction of the Lord to write this book, the hours just flew by, and before I knew it, the day was spent and I had more and more of the book written.

I never got to go overseas with Burnie Davis. Upon returning from India, he called me and asked if I would like to meet him for coffee at a local restaurant. I was excited to go meet him and hear all the awesome things that God had done. We sat across from each other at the Village Inn in Pueblo—which, by the way, is still there and I always think of Burnie every time I go there. Burnie told me of the miraculous healings and miracles that God had done and how he would have loved for me to be there with him. I told him what the Lord had told me about preaching first in our city and then going out from there eventually to all the world. Burnie always told me, "Tim, all you need is a miracle under your belt, and you will never be the same!" I had no idea that morning would be the last time I would get to sit with Burnie, have a cup of coffee, listen to his stories, or go anywhere with him again.

The next day was Sunday, and during the morning service, I saw Burnie get up out of his seat and head for his office. Burnie had a private office at the church. I noticed that he seemed to be hunched over a bit as he walked. I saw his wife Dolly get up and follow him, along with an usher. The pastor was preaching and not too many seemed to notice them getting up and going to the office. I got up out of my seat and walked around the back of the sanctuary to his office door. I knocked and the usher opened the door and said to come in quickly. Burnie was on the floor having a massive heart attack! Just then, I heard the sirens and ambulance pull up to his private exit door. I began praying in other tongues as they loaded him into the ambulance. I rushed to the hospital, as several others did. We waited to hear how Burnie was doing, only to hear the news that he had passed away.

My heart was crushed. Thinking more of myself at the moment, I thought that Burnie was the only person, other than my wife Peggy, who really believed in me at the time. He believed I was called of God to be an Evangelist and took the time to impart things into my life, and now he was gone. That was 1987, 32 years ago. The influence that Burnie had on my life and on Peggy has never left us. When I met Burnie in 1985, I had no idea who he was and what all God had done through his life and ministry. He believed in me and what he imparted into my life has extended into my ministry all of these years.

I felt it beneficial to share this story in hopes of helping someone to realize that we don't have to make mistakes to learn a lesson, but if you do, always know that God is there to walk you through. Also, I hope that this story of Burnie and me (I could write many other stories about him) will inspire someone to realize that God places us in the path of great men and women to be examples and help disciple us if we will humble ourselves and submit to their anointing and gift. They may look like just another person on the outside or seem less important than someone we hope to meet someday, but know that God is ready to mark your life in a way that cannot be marked without His touch through others He brings across our path. I met a "man" named Burnie, I found my "mission," and God helped me recover from my "mistake!"

22

MEET ME FOR DRINKS

THAT SAME YEAR, while on a commercial job for a number of weeks, I got to know several of the men I was working around on the job site. They were all rough and dirty-mouthed, but I was accustomed to that growing up around construction all my life. I made it clear that I was a Christian and a preacher. I never pushed anything on the guys or preached at them; however, I never shied away from the fact that I was a believer. If they asked me what I thought, I would tell them straight up. There were times when these guys would ask or say things in an attempt to get me to argue with them or get angry. They would try to rattle me. I am reminded of what Jesus said: *"Behold, I send you out as sheep in the midst of wolves. Therefore be wise as serpents and harmless as doves"* (Matthew 10:16 NKJV).

It was getting toward the end of the workday and there were a couple of guys working closest to me on a long wall we were building. One turned to the other (I was between them) and said, "Hey, don't you think it's Grisham's turn to buy the beer after work?" The other guy said, "I think you're right," and turned to me and said, "Grisham, it's almost Beer:30 and we decided you're buying!" It was Friday, and when whistle blew for quitting time, everyone on the job called it Beer:30. I had two responses in this situation. I could have gotten offended and made sure they knew that I was a Christian and didn't drink beer anymore. I could have used that moment as an opportunity to preach a little hell fire to them, especially as they had been giving me and another Christian guy a hard time. The other Christian worker would leave the group at lunch time, eat his lunch alone, and read his Bible. Nothing wrong with that, but it made it more difficult to witness to the rest of the crew. The guys loved to ridicule him and make fun of him. He never said a word. Again, that's fine, but in the four to five months we worked together, I never saw him say hello to anyone. He just ignored everyone. I even tried to eat lunch with him one day, but he let me know he was a certain denomination and did not agree with my brand of Christianity. Not only did I have challenges in sharing my beliefs with my co-workers, even the "Christian" co-workers didn't want to speak with me.

The whistle blew; we all grabbed our tools and started to climb down the scaffolding. The two guys both hollered at me, "Grisham, are you going to buy the beer?" I knew if I told them I didn't drink, they would get a good laugh out of it and leave. But the Holy Ghost stirred in me and I said, "I don't drink beer," and they started in on me, so I continued, "Wait a minute. How about some wine?" They both looked at each other and made comments that I was one of those types of preachers. Comments like, "Doesn't the Bible say something about being a wine bibber or something like that?" I said, "You guys want a drink or not?" "Sure, we will have a couple drinks of your wine. What kind do you have?" I simply said, "It's called new wine." Of course, they had never heard of that brand of wine. I told them to follow me to my truck and I would pull it out so they can have a few drinks.

They followed me with tools in hand to the back of my truck. I reached in and grabbed my Bible. When I pulled the

Bible out of the truck, I held it up, acted like I was unscrewing a cap, and proceeded to tip my head back and take a big drink. Then I reached my Bible out toward them both and said, "Jesus will save you and give you a drink of His Spirit that will cause you to never thirst again!" I was ready for them to burst out laughing, when to my surprise, both of their heads dropped and one of the guys started crying! I looked at him and said, "Jesus loves you, man. You need to let Him come into your life."

He told me that he used to live for the Lord and then had turned away. He acknowledged that he needed to live like he used to. He turned to the guy next to him and said, "Will you forgive me?" The other said, "What for?" He said that he'd been a terrible example as a Christian to the man and that he was going to ask the Lord to forgive him. He told his friend that they needed to give their lives to Jesus. He asked him to pray with him. I was shocked! I stood there and watched as these guys prayed together, asking Jesus to come into their lives. Then they looked up and thanked me for not being ashamed of Christ and being an example of someone who really was following Jesus. I asked if I could pray with them both, and they agreed. We all three joined hands as I prayed for them. Once again, I realized that while I did not really enjoy having to work a secular job, the Lord was with me and His desire was to work through me to reach others with the Good News of the Gospel!

23

TRUNK LOAD OF DONUTS

FOR A NUMBER OF YEARS, I spent the majority of my Friday, and sometimes Saturday, nights out witnessing on the streets of my hometown of Pueblo, Colorado. The more time you spend going on purpose to share Christ with others, the more opportunities you will have to experience supernatural results! It always amazes me how some people (Christians) say they want to see the power of God or ask why we don't see more of God's power manifested in the church. Yet, rarely if ever, do they step out and do what Jesus instructed them as believers to do.

I used to hear it quite frequently: "Why don't we see more healings and miracles and salvations in the church?" The answer is simply that Jesus <u>never</u> said, "When you have church, these signs will follow." No, He said in Matthew (10:7-8, AMP), *"And as you go, preach, saying, 'The kingdom of heaven is at hand.' Heal the sick, raise the dead, cleanse the lepers, cast out demons. Freely you have received, freely give."* All we have to do is read the Bible and we will see that most all salvations, healings, miracles, signs, and wonders are recorded outside the walls of the church. It was that way in Jesus' ministry and His disciples' ministries.

It was just another Friday, and as was my custom, I arrived at the church at 5:30am to unlock the doors and get ready for early morning prayer. When I was on staff, the staff was required to be at early morning prayer from 5:30am to 6:30am. The church was open for community prayer from 6:30-7:30am. When prayer was finished, I would walk around the corner from the church and get a cup of coffee and sometimes a donut from the Daylight Donuts shop.

While waiting in line, I noticed that they had some day-old donuts on the shelf for a discounted price. I thought to myself that I should buy those donuts and take them with me to the streets that night and give them out. I asked if they had anymore day-olds I could buy, as there were only a couple dozen on the shelf. The owner told me that was all that she had at that time. She asked me how many I wanted. I told her what I wanted to do, and she told me to come back later that afternoon for more. I told her I'd come back during my lunch hour. I returned at noon and the owner brought out a large clear plastic bag about the size of a thirty-gallon trash bag full of different kinds of donuts. That's a lot of donuts! I wasn't prepared to purchase so many at one time.

I told her I wasn't sure that I had enough money to buy all of the donuts she had. She told me not to worry and that the donuts were "on the house." She had decided to make some extra donuts that day and give them to me because she wanted to be part of what I was doing. She wanted to be part of giving back. She asked me if I was going to do this every week. I explained to her that this was my first time sharing Jesus while handing out donuts. She let me know that she would like to be part of this again, if I choose to do this again. She said she would save the extras and give them to me each week. Wow, all from one idea! I had not even had the chance to do anything and the Lord provided me with a trunk load of donuts!

That night, I put the large bag of donuts in the trunk of my 1968 Mustang fastback (wish I still had that car) and I headed to the downtown area of Pueblo. After driving around for a while, it seemed like there were not that many people on the streets. As soon as I asked God where to find the people, I heard the Holy Spirit instruct me to turn and go down a specific alley. I've noticed in my life so many times that when the Holy Spirit speaks to me, it's easy to dismiss the voice as just a passing thought in my head. I have learned to take a moment and listen inward where the Holy Spirit dwells. *"By this we know that we abide in Him, and He in us, because He has given us of His Spirit"* (1 John 4:13 NKJV). The Holy Spirit is there with us to help us. *"But when the Helper comes, whom I shall send to you from the Father, the Spirit of truth who proceeds from the Father, He will testify of Me"* (John 15:26 NKJV).

As I heard this inward voice, I listened and drove down the alley. I was alone that night and it was around 10:30pm. My natural mind was telling me that this "looks iffy" and I should probably not go down the alley. I literally had just turned down the alley, and behind a vacant building parking lot, a party was going on. There had to be about fifty young people tailgating; all of them were hanging out, drinking, and drugging. The strong odor of pot was in the air. When I pulled around the corner, my headlights caused a panic and the crowd began to scatter. I shut my lights off quickly and turned the engine off. Once they saw that it was a Mustang and not a cop car, they settled down.

I sat there in my car thinking. *What do I do, Lord? There is a huge group of kids out here partying and I am by myself.* The Holy Ghost said, "You are not by yourself. I am with you always, even to the end." I remember, as though it were yesterday, fear trying to grip me and my mind full of thoughts of why this was not a good idea to get out of the car. Then that voice on the inside, the Holy Ghost, said, "How would you like to walk on water tonight? If you will step out of your car and begin walking toward this group of people (who by now were not paying any attention to me sitting there), I will show you what it is like to walk on the water." In complete trust and faith, I got out of my car and walked toward the gathering of people. I had gotten their attention as they were looking at me. I'm sure they were wondering what this long-haired thirty-something guy was doing.

I stood there for what seemed like an eternity, not saying a word. Then a guy wearing a high school letterman jacket stepped out and said, "What's up? Are you a Narc or some-thing?" I told them that I wasn't. I told them I was a preacher and God had sent me there to give them all a message. Now several other guys from the football team stepped forward and others in the crowd began laughing. One guy said, "Is this some kind of a joke, man?" Another saying, "Here, you want a beer?" I told them no and explained again that I was there to deliver a message to them from God.

By this time, I had even more of the group's attention. They were probably thinking I was crazy. My mind was racing with thoughts of *What do I say? What do I do now, Lord?* and more. The group began to settle down and gather around me. Then I spoke up. "I am here tonight because God sent me here. To be honest, I would rather be home with my beautiful wife and kids, but instead I am standing in a parking lot with a bunch of people I don't even know. God wants you to know tonight that because He loves you so much, He has sent me to tell you in person."

I noticed several of the guys standing directly in front of me putting their beers down to their sides. "Tonight, you all have an opportunity to receive a gift from God and that gift is His eternal life that is only found in Jesus Christ His Son. Jesus died for every one of you, including me, and it was not so we could become religious, but so we could be set free from sin and death. Jesus is not dead. He is alive because God raised Him up and He wants to give you the gift of salvation and eternal life. All you are required to do is believe and receive Him by asking Him into your heart."

You could have heard a pin drop in that alley! Every person's head was down, with the exception of a couple. I heard one say, "I am out of here. This guy is some sort of religious nut!" I boldly continued, "Is there any of you here that will step out from this crowd and say yes to Jesus?" The guy in the letterman jacket stepped forward without hesitation. Then a couple of the other guys did the same. I asked again if anyone else wanted to ask Jesus into their lives. Hands began to pop up all over that dark alley.

I continued, "God is very pleased with your decision. Let's pray." Heads were bowed as I led them through a prayer and each of them spoke the words. I can't begin to tell you the rush of anointing and the peace and presence of God that flooded that parking lot that night. I will never forget it. After we all prayed, I gave a few of them a hug. I encouraged them to get a Bible and read it, to go to church, and if they did not know where to go, I could point them in the right direction. Then I invited them to come to my car. I popped open my trunk and opened the bag of donuts. I heard one or two of them yell, "This guy has free donuts over here!"

After that night, for several months, I took donuts that were given to me by the donut shop out to the streets. The donuts became a real hit for a while and helped me make a connection with those who hung out on the streets of our downtown. God has a way to reach people and a way to connect with them if we will just be ready and willing to go.

24

THE TRUTH ABOUT SANTA

WHILE SERVING on staff in 1988 at Church on the Rock in Pueblo, it was decided by the Sr. Pastor that all the men on staff would go to the mountains for a time of prayer and fasting. At that time, there were five men on staff. Up until this time, I had only fasted a day or two, maybe three at the most. Pastor told us that we were going for seven days of prayer and fasting. We all agreed to go; however, there really wasn't a choice at the time; being on staff, it was a requirement to go.

In today's world, or at least among some of the church people I know, that type of requirement would not fly. In those days and today, I believe in submitting to the authorities God has set over us. When it comes to the church, the pastor is the one God has set in a position of authority to lead the flock. If you agree to take a position, whether you are paid or not, you should be ready and willing to follow the directions given. This is sound advice for anyone who may be serving in a church and have a position of responsibility. This holds true even if you're volunteering or involved in the ministry of helps as taught in 1 Corinthians:

"So God has appointed and placed in the church [for His own use]: first apostles [chosen by Christ], second prophets [those who foretell the future, those who speak a new message from God to the people], third teachers, then those who work miracles, then those with the gifts of healings, **the helpers**, the administrators, and speakers in various kinds of [unknown] tongues." (1 Corinthians 12:28 AMP)

God sets those in the church with the gift of helps. I share this Scripture and thoughts to help anyone reading this to understand about authority and why going on a prayer/fasting trip for seven days was important. I didn't argue, because I understood and respected the authority of my pastor.

It was wintertime and we were in a small house in the mountains of Colorado. It was cold with lots of snow on the ground. We primarily spent our time inside the small house for seven days. We had water to drink and no food. We spent hours praying together, as well as hours alone in our respective rooms, praying and reading the Word. We had no TV, radio, internet, or cell phone. I wonder how many Christians could even fast from their smartphone or the internet for seven days, let alone do it without food and only water to drink.

When we began this time of fasting and prayer, I had an expectation to hear from God. I was seeking the Lord for direction at that time, direction for my life, and direction for ministry. Yes, I was on staff as an evangelist; however, it seemed like I was the all-around handyman more than anything else. My efforts to bring the church into a place of being outreach-minded and stepping out into different types of outreach ministry was a challenge. Back in those days, it seemed as though most, not all, but most Christians were on a mission to find out how to get their needs met, how to get blessed or healed, and how to prosper. All of these things are important to God and they are part of the new covenant in Christ; however,

Christians tended to be self-minded instead of outreach-minded.

The week seemed to drag on and on. The days got longer and longer the hungrier I got. On the third day, my body began to experience a lot of pain. It was becoming more and more difficult to sleep at night. Day after day, I was waiting to have some grand revelation from God, some supernatural experience. I wanted to hear the voice of God tell me to get up from this place, go eat pizza, and there you will meet a man and he will prophesy the oracles of God, or something like that! I wanted a supernatural experience. I was hungry, missing my wife, missing my kids.

By the end of the seventh day, I was so excited to leave that place, to get home, to see my wife and kids, and to GO EAT! I remember the thirty-minute drive from the mountain town of Beulah, Colorado, back to the church in Pueblo. Everyone talked about what they felt the Lord was saying or what they got out of this time of prayer and fasting. I remember being somewhat disappointed because I really did not feel like I had benefited from this time, especially given the pain I felt and the lack of sleep. Little did I realize what God was really doing in me at that time. Even thirty years later, as I reflect back on that time, I cannot say that it was necessary for me to fast seven days to get the results that I later realized God had done. It was a good exercise of self-discipline and taking control over my flesh.

Several days after the fast, the Holy Spirit began speaking to me about dressing up as Santa and going into the bars and nightclubs of our city. I had even had some of these thoughts during the fast, but just ignored them, as I was seeking something in my mind much more spiritual. When the thoughts would come, I would rebuke them and push them aside.

Santa and I had a history at this point. I had gotten so tired of the commercialism of Christmas. It was just after Thanksgiving when we went on this fast. I was feeling the financial pressure of Christmas coming on. With each year and having small children, it never seemed like we had enough money when Christmas rolled around. I had gotten a religious, self-righteous attitude about the Christmas season. I blamed society for taking the real meaning of Christmas and making it into some kind of commercialistic, greedy, selfish holiday that I did not want to participate in any longer. I even went as far that year to try and convince my wife Peggy that we should not even get a Christmas tree because it was just a pagan thing.

I had a Mr. Scrooge attitude about Christmas, and thoughts of dressing up as Santa Claus and going to the bars and night-clubs to tell people about Jesus are coming to my mind. I was determined that there was NO WAY I was going to do such a thing. I grew up as a child of the '60s and my parents told us kids all about Santa and how he came and put presents under the tree on Christmas Eve. I am sure you're familiar with the whole story and the song "Santa Claus is Coming to Town": "You'd better watch out, better not cry / You'd better not pout, I'm telling you why / Santa Claus is coming to town." My parents would use this as a means of discipline the closer Christmas got. I'm sure it was because the closer it got to Christmas, the rottener I became as a kid! Then the verse, "He's making a list and checking it twice, He's gonna find out who's naughty and nice" would bring fear, because I was certain Santa was not going to bring me what I wanted. I was convinced as an adult that the Santa in these lyrics was just a way for parents to lie and manipulate their children over the Christmas holidays to try and deal with their misbehavior.

Thanksgiving Day 1967, I was eight years old and we lived at 627 Tyler Street in Pueblo, Colorado. My mom was working feverishly to get the turkey out of the oven and dinner on the table. We had our dining table set up in the living room and a couple of small card tables for me and my sister, along with the cousins who would be coming. I had been thinking about Christmas and watching commercials on TV about the latest toys from Mattel. There was a vacuum operated machine that made plastic bugs and critters. I remember, even at eight, wondering how Santa makes toys if they are already being sold at the store by a company. Did Santa make them in his work-shop, then take them to the store, or is he so busy that he has to go to the store and buy toys from the store?

My mom was trying to get dinner on, company was showing up to eat soon, and I was asking her 101 questions about Santa Claus. Finally, she turned to me in frustration and said, "You need to stop asking me all these questions!" I wanted to know. How did Santa get toys into our house when we don't have a chimney for him to come down? My mom asked if I really wanted to know the truth about Santa Claus. Of course, I did. She said, "Honey, he is not real. It is just a story. There is not a real Santa Claus. Now go play and let me get dinner on the table." What a let down. From that day, I decided that Santa Claus, the Easter Bunny, the Tooth Fairy, and every other imag-inary character that parents tell their kids about were a hoax. I was crushed at the thought that Santa, of all people, was not real! I could understand the Easter Bunny or Tooth Fairy, but not Santa.

All of these memories and my current situation at the time were culminating in my mind when the Lord prompted me to go dress up as Santa and go to the bars and nightclubs. I thought of every excuse or way out of dressing up. There was no way this could be the voice of God I was hearing. There were churches on every corner, 24-hour Christian program-ming on TV, Christian bookstores, Christian radio, and more. If someone really wants to know about Jesus, they can go to church like I do or even go to Bible college. Then the people in those bars... they are just sinners and don't want to hear about Jesus.

See, my opinion of people who hung out in bars and night-clubs, smoked cigarettes, smoked dope, and took drugs was not very good. I felt as though they made their bed, so they could just sleep in it. I really had very little, if any compassion, for people like that. The truth of the matter was, I became one of those people for a few years out of high school and in my first few months of being married. I was being a self-righteous hypocrite, and truth be known, the idea of going into these places filled me with fear and shame.

I know this is a long story, but I believe there are some important things that might help someone reading this. I wrestled with God over the idea of a Santa outreach, trying to convince myself it's the devil trying to set me up. Then one Sunday morning, just a week or two before Christmas, a lady in the church came up to me before service and said, "Brother Tim, can I talk to you for a minute?" She continued, "I am so excited. God spoke to me this week to give you something and you're going to be so surprised!" I thought to myself, *Praise God!* I was believing for a number of things, especially after the fast I had been on a few weeks earlier. I thought it was going to pay off!

We agreed to meet after church so she could give me the surprise. It seemed like the longest service ever. All I could think about was what Mary was going to give me. Service was finally over; I tried to act calm and unexcited. I followed her out to her car; she popped open the trunk of her car. What could it be? She reached in and grabbed a large box in a bag. She pulled the box out and there it was... a brand new, never opened box containing a Santa Claus suit! I could not believe it! NO!

I did my best to be thankful, but really, all I could think about was that there was no way God was gifting this Santa suit to me. Mary said, "Brother Tim, the Lord told me to give this to you. It's brand new." She went on to explain that she and her husband bought it and he was going to dress as Santa for their small children at Christmas, but then they felt like they did not want to do that after all. She, with excitement in her voice, asked, "What are you going to do with it?" Before any words could come out, she said, "Are you going to burn it?" I thought to myself that burning it was a good idea. It was customary to burn records, tapes, magazines, posters, or anything else that was ungodly during that time. We did not want to be a part of influencing others and did not want to take a chance of just throwing it in the trash and someone finding it. I told her I would let her know what I was going to do with the suit and thanked her. I remember walking away really knowing in my heart what the Lord wanted me to do, but still trying to find a way out of it.

25

CHRISTMAS 1988, HERE COMES SANTA

I FINALLY SUBMITTED to the idea of dressing like Santa and going into the bars. I spent a lot of time praying and asking the Lord what to do. The Holy Spirit gave me some simple instructions to follow and told me to design a special Christmas tract. Along with the tract, the Holy Spirit also told me to buy large candy canes and attach the tracts to the candy canes with ribbon. I wanted to buy the little tiny candy canes, but the Lord specifically said the large ones. I got some friends to come over, as well as Peggy, to help fold the tracts, punch holes with a paper punch, and tie the tracts to the candy canes. We even went as far as to make the ribbon curl like you do on gift wrapping. It was, and is, a tedious process. We have spent hundreds of hours over the years doing this.

The time had come. It was Saturday night and Christmas Eve. I loaded up my Santa bag with tracts and candy canes and met up with a friend who had volunteered to go with me from church. We prayed and I told him what the Holy Spirit instructed me to do. I was instructed to go in the door of the bar and head straight for the back of the building. I wasn't to hand out any candy canes until we got to the back. He asked me why.

I told him I didn't know why, but it was what the Lord instructed.

The first bar we stopped at was full and we didn't go in. I was trying to wrap my mind around the crazy thoughts of what was about to happen. Were they going to throw me out the door? Take me to the back alley and rip my Santa suit off, leaving me beat up and bloody? All kinds of vain imaginations were trying to grip my heart and bring fear. I did what the Bible says in 2 Corinthians:

> "The weapons we use in our fight are not the world's weapons but God's powerful weapons, which we use to destroy strongholds. We destroy false arguments; we pull down every proud obstacle that is raised against the knowledge of God; we take every thought captive and make it obey Christ." (2 Corinthians 10:4-5 GNB)

I like how this Scripture reads in the Good News Bible version. Look at that last sentence: take every thought captive and make it obey Christ. That is how we are to live our lives for Christ, taking every thought that is contrary to the truth and casting them down and making our thoughts obey the Word and obey the truth. The New King James Version reads, *"casting down arguments and every high thing that exalts itself against the knowledge of God, bringing every thought into captivity to the obedience of Christ."* The devil is a liar and the father of lies, according to Jesus in John 8:44, and he tries his best to throw thoughts of fear and worry our way, but we must resist him in faith. *"Therefore submit to God. Resist the devil and he will flee from you"* (James 4:7 NKJV).

I turned to my friend as we stood at the door of the tavern and asked, "Are you ready?" He replied, "Yeah, dude, let's do it!" My friend was newly saved and had recently gotten off of drugs. He was calm and ready to go. I was fighting fear, overcoming vain thoughts, and felt like I was going into the lion's den! I opened the door, took a step inside, and it seemed everyone in the bar turned to see who just came in. All of a sudden, people began to burst out hollering, "Hey, it's Santa!" I remembered what the Holy Spirit told me about going to the back of the bar first. People were smiling and asking, "Hey, Santa, what did you bring me?" I stayed focused on the back of the room, maneuvering around tables, and people reaching out to give me a pat on the back. I started thinking, *Maybe this is not so bad after all. Everyone seems to like Santa!* Then the negative thought came: *You just wait until you give them the candy cane and they read the tract. They will know what you're up to and throw you out.* Again, I cast down that thought and moved forward. I got to the back and turned around to realize why the Lord told me to do it that way. I had everybody's attention; I couldn't get out of there without giving a candy cane to every person. God knows what He is doing. I probably would have stepped in the door, handed a couple of tracts out, and left the place before anyone could realize what I was up to. The truth was that I was dealing with fear and shame.

Paul the Apostle said this in Romans 1:16 (NKJV): *"For I am not ashamed of the gospel of Christ, for it is the power of God to salvation for everyone who believes, for the Jew first and also for the Greek."*

Paul faced great criticism and persecution and even death, yet, he never gave in to fear or shame. Shame is just a byproduct of fear and pride; Jesus said these words in Mark 8:38 (NKJV): *"For whoever is ashamed of Me and My words in this adulterous and sinful generation, of him the Son of Man also will be ashamed when He comes in the glory of His Father with the holy angels."*

Thank God we are not left to stand for Christ on our own ability, our own strength, and our own wisdom. That is why Jesus sent the gift of the Holy Spirit on the day of Pentecost, to empower believers in Christ. We have the greater One living in us to help us and give us power to be His witnesses.

> "Therefore do not be ashamed of the testimony of our Lord, nor of me His prisoner, but share with me in the sufferings for the gospel according to the power of God." (1 Timothy 1:8 NKJV)

I was standing in the back of the bar while everyone was wondering what Santa has in his sack. I looked over at my friend and he was already passing out his bag of candy canes and tracts. With a big HO-HO-HO and a Merry Christmas, I began handing out my Gospel candy canes. I was actually shocked at the reception we were getting, people asking me what the little paper was about. I would tell them to read it and that it tells them how to have the best Christmas ever. I would tell them that there was a free gift offer that is out of this world on the inside.

As I made my way back toward the door, I was just about to grab the knob when I heard someone say, "Hey, Santa, I did not get one of those things you're handing out." It was the bartender and owner of the tavern. I had almost made it out and now the owner wants a candy cane. If he read it and found out what this was all about, we were in trouble. As you know, this was not the Holy Spirit giving me these thoughts; it was my own fear, and the devil trying to torment me. I kept reminding myself of what Paul told Timothy: *"For God has not given us a spirit of fear, but of power and of love and of a sound mind"* (2 Timothy 1:7 NKJV).

I handed the bartender a Gospel candy cane and then turned toward the door. He said, "Hey, wait a minute, Santa. Stay for a drink. It's on the house." With some quick wit, I told him that Santa can't drink and drive. He laughed and offered me a Coke or 7UP. I heard the Holy Spirit tell me to stay. I sat down at the bar and he handed me a glass with Coca-Cola and one of those tiny straws. As I sat and drank my Coke through that straw, trying not to mess up my beard, the bartender stood back in the light of the Rocky Mountain Coors sign and began reading the tract. I was sucking on that straw so hard, trying to finish my soda before he realized what the tract was about, that I was getting one of those brain freezes. I always call them ice cream headaches.

He put the tract and candy cane down on the bar, leaned toward me, and said, "Are you some kind of preacher?" To be honest, the thought ran through my mind at that moment to say no, but there was no way I was going to deny the Lord. I am not ashamed of who I am and Who I represent! As a believer, we stand up for Christ, resist the fear, resist shame, resist our own flesh, and resist the devil trying to influence us. When we do this, the anointing in us rises up and there comes a boldness that cannot be compared to anything else.

I said, "Yes, sir, I am a preacher of the Gospel, a Christian." He asked what church I was from, so I told him where I went to church. I told him that I was here to share Jesus and His love for him and everyone else. He took a step back, stood there for a moment, and said, "I thought you people were too good to come into a place like this and talk to people like us." I replied, "Well, I don't know about others, but as for myself and my friend over there (who, by the way, was praying for an older couple to receive forgiveness and come back into a real relationship with Jesus), we believe God has sent us here to tell you He loves you right where you are. He loves you so much that He sent a guy dressed like Santa to get your attention."

We must never forget that Jesus came into the world not to condemn people in their sin! In John 3:17 (NKJV), Jesus says, *"For God did not send His Son into the world to condemn the world, but that the world through Him might be saved."* Paul says in 1 Timothy 1:15 (NKJV), *"This is a faithful saying and worthy of all acceptance, that Christ Jesus came into the world to save sinners, of whom I am chief."* Again, in Romans 5:8 (NKJV), Paul says, *"But God demonstrates His own love toward us, in that while we were still sinners, Christ died for us."*

The man behind the bar looked at me with tears welling up in his eyes and said, "I never thought you people cared for people like us." I told him that we did, and more importantly, that God does. He asked, "See that table over in the far corner on the left?" I said, "Yes." He said, "That's your table. I am going to make that your place when you come, and I will send people to you who need help." I was blown away! That night, I experienced yet another level of God's love being poured out. I prayed for the bartender to come to know Christ in a deeper and more personal way. The bartender told me that he had been saved many years ago, but just didn't stick with it.

People all over are needing to know Jesus, not just about Him. They need a relationship, not a religion. As we left that tavern, I was overflowing with the love of God, so excited to have overcome the fear that tried to torment me for weeks about doing what has become known as "My Santa Outreach." That night, we went to bar after bar passing out hundreds of Gospel candy canes and sharing Jesus, the greatest gift. That was Christmas Eve 1988.

It has now been over thirty years since I went into my first bar dressed as Santa. Since 1988 it has been my joy to dress as Santa each year and visit many bars and nightclubs all over the US and several countries around the world. Each year, passing out our candy canes and Santa gospel tracts, praying with people to receive Christ, laying hands on the sick and operating in the gifts of the Spirit. Watching God change lives right before our eyes!

26

THREE MEN IN ROBES

MANY OF MY stories are of times when I purposed to go out and share Jesus with others. I have found over the years that if you're going to take Jesus at His Word, then you have to be willing and obedient to step out and do something. Jesus said to a couple of fisherman, "Follow Me and I will make you fishers of men." If we just sit around waiting for something to happen, chances are it won't, but if something does happen, more than likely, we will miss it because we are not looking purposefully.

Jesus said something to His disciples that has spoken to me many times over the years. In John 4, Jesus says, *"Behold, I say to you, lift up your eyes and look at the fields, for they are already white for harvest!"* As I go into the details of this story, I encourage you to read the account of the woman at the well and when Jesus met her there. Jesus told His disciples, "Lift up your eyes and look!" That is something we have to do on purpose. We have to give attention to our surroundings and to the people around us, or like the disciples, we will just go about our daily lives missing the opportunities that are there. There are times when God is telling us to do something and we miss the point of what He is saying like the disciples did. In John 4, He sent them for food, but Jesus was talking about food, as in doing the will of God. John 4:38 (NKJV): *"I sent you to reap that for which you have not labored; others have labored, and you have entered into their labors."* Jesus sent them on a mission, but they thought they were just going to go buy some food. How many times we can miss a divine appointment because we are preoccupied with the natural things of life.

One day as I arrived at work, I was laying brick on a house just outside of town in the country. There were three men putting siding up on the back of the house. These guys were wearing ankle length robes made of denim. I had seen others wearing similar robes here and there on different job sites. The men all had long hair and beards, similar to the look from the hippy days. I did not know who they were or what they believed, and to be honest, I never tried to find out. I just thought they were a bit weird.

That day when I took a break to eat my lunch, I heard the Holy Spirit speak. When I say I hear the Holy Spirit, most of the time, it is an unction on the inside—just a knowing. I hear God's voice on the inside, not with my natural ears. I would compare it to when you know on the inside you should not do something, or your conscience tells you that you better not do another thing. That is what it is like for me when I say I hear the Lord, God, or the Holy Spirit "speak."

I am getting ready to eat when the Holy Spirit says that He wants me to talk to these guys about Him. Again, especially years ago, I would have this argument that would go on in my head. I would go back and forth with the Lord, giving one excuse after another why I did not want to do what He was telling me to do. The three men asked if they could sit in the garage where I was and join me for lunch. I told them to have a seat. How easy was that; they came to me. I ate my lunch, the whole time hearing that voice on the inside saying, "Talk to them while they are eating."

Soon lunch was over; they got up and left to go back outside to work. I missed it! I did not step out and do what the Lord was telling me to do. I felt bad and guilty. I was kicking myself for not speaking up. Those kinds of feelings are not from the Lord, by the way. God does not condemn us when we disobey or miss it, but He does correct us. Look here for a moment: *"For if our heart condemns us, God is greater than our heart, and knows all things"* (1 John 3:20 NKJV). Jesus did not condemn His disciples in John 4 when they missed it, but He did instruct them and correct them. So here I am thinking that I really missed it, so I prayed and asked the Lord to give me another opportunity with these guys.

Later that afternoon, I took a break to get a cold drink and a snack. Once again, these guys came around to where I was in the garage where it was much cooler. The temperature that day was well above the 90-degree mark. Before I could say anything, they began to gather up their tools and load their truck. I asked if they were done for the day and they said they were finished with the job and headed to another. I knew that my opportunity was almost gone. Before I knew it, they were almost finished loading their tools. I needed to act fast.

I walked around to the other side of the house, wondering what to say. I heard the engine start up and their truck pulled away. I had missed my chance. As I watched them drive off, I felt like a failure. I had not followed the Holy Spirit's leading. I went back to work. I asked myself what I would do if they came back for some reason. I prayed and asked the Lord to send them back somehow.

About fifteen minutes later, I heard a sound. I stepped around the corner of the house and saw dust flying up in the air as a vehicle was coming down the dirt road. I wondered who was coming down the road? Duh! I had just prayed about fifteen minutes ago asking the Lord to send these guys back! It was them. They came flying up the road, pulled into the drive-way, and one of the guys jumped out of the truck. I was surprised. I asked, "You back already?" The guy who jumped out of the truck replied, "Yeah, we forgot one of our electrical extension cords." As he began rolling up this cord, I knew the Lord had sent them back. Yes, they had forgotten one of their extension cords, but I had prayed and asked the Holy Spirit to send them back. I knew this was my opportunity once again.

I don't remember exactly what I said to the guy, but it was a pretty weak witness. I did not talk to them about a relationship with Jesus. I remember the guy's response to me was that the men believed in the name Yahweh and not the name Jesus. Our conversation did not last but a few moments and then they left. What I learned that day more than anything else is how much God desires to reach people through us. God will work things out to our advantage if we will just step out. He will literally turn people around and send them back! Regardless of what their reason was for coming back, I knew the Lord brought them back for me to talk to. I know I did not fully do what the Lord asked me to do that day. In my opinion, I missed it, but I have never forgotten that day because it reminds me not that I missed it, but that I am not going to give in to the fear of not knowing what to say. Jesus said this: *"For I will give you a mouth and wisdom, which all your adversaries shall not be able to gainsay nor resist"* (Luke 21:15 KJV). I have learned over time that you can trust the Holy Spirit to give you the words to speak, if you will trust Him and speak up. Jesus said in Matthew 10:19-20 (GNB):

> "When they bring you to trial, do not worry about what you are going to say or how you will say it; when the time comes, you will be given what you will say. For the words you will speak will not be yours; they will come from the Spirit of your Father speaking through you."

While you or I may not be brought to trial for our witness, the devil loves to make us feel that way sometimes when we want to share Christ with others. You may feel like you're being put on the stand, so to speak, but know that the Holy Spirit will always give you the words to speak.

27

LAST BUT NOT LEAST

I HAVE ONLY JUST BEGUN to share my personal, but super-natural, encounters in this book. I look forward to sharing many more in future volumes. While writing these stories, my mind was flooded with memories of one encounter after another. I'm reminded of God's love for others and His amazing grace. We are privileged to be His ambassadors of Good News. *"Now then, we are ambassadors for Christ, as though God were pleading through us: we implore you on Christ's behalf, be reconciled to God"* (2 Corinthians 5:20 NKJV).

In this last story I am sharing, it is my hope that these testimonies will serve to inspire you to trust the Holy Spirit in you to live big through you!

Back in 1994, I had been asked by a missionary friend to come to Romania. He had moved from Germany to Romania to begin a new work there and I was excited to go. In those days, I would fly from the United States to Amsterdam, Holland, then on to Budapest, Hungary. Once I arrived in Hungary, we would drive from Budapest to Cluj, Romania. Back then, it was a tough eight-hour drive, the roads were littered with holes, and it was just all-around bad driving conditions. There were no places to stop along the way to eat or use the bathroom, except for a town about halfway, and it was always a blessing to stop there.

I felt a real connection to Romania my first trip, even though the country was going through very difficult times, as it had been through a revolution just a few years prior. I would see people standing in line to buy bread and stores had little to offer in the way of groceries. The faces of the people didn't seem to show much of any emotion, especially joy.

Not long after my first trip, I made plans to go back. This time, I invited Bill, a youth pastor friend of mine, to come along. This was his first trip out of the United States and on foreign soil, so everything was new for him. When we landed in Budapest, Hungary, the plane taxied and parked on the tarmac. There, they would unload the passengers and you would be escorted from the plane into the airport customs area. It was a little intimidating. They would have you walk single file between two yellow lines painted on the pavement. Along the way were military personnel with rifles in hand standing guard. Once inside, it was dark, gloomy, and dirty. Nothing like today, whatsoever; in fact, today, many of the international airports around the world far exceed our international airports in the United States.

We walked from the plane to the customs secured area in the airport. Once inside the building, it was not much warmer inside than outside. As we waited in line, I noticed there were four or five custom agent booths, but only two were open and everyone was standing in line at the same one. I wondered why people didn't move over to the second booth. I asked my friend that question. About that time, I looked up and saw a small sign above the booth. Written in Hungarian, I was unable to read the sign; however, I did notice in small letters in English, the words: *Ambassadors and Dignitaries.* My friend told me what I had just read. I told him, "We are in the wrong line, then." He asked me what I meant, and I told him to follow me, we were getting into the right line. Bill told me that we couldn't go through that line as we weren't ambassadors. I told him that we were according to 2 Corinthians 5:20: *"We are ambassadors for Christ!"*

I went straight over to the booth for ambassadors, as no one was waiting in line, and I stepped up to the little window and handed my passport to the attendant. He looked at me, looked at my passport, and looked as though he was about to send me back to the line I had just left, when I said, "I am an Ambassador for Christ." He stamped my passport and said, "You go." Praise God, we were through customs and way ahead of that line and that cold waiting area.

I had a revelation that day; I saw myself the way the Word of God describes me, as an ambassador, a Christ representative. Webster's Dictionary says this about the word ambassador: an official envoy; especially, a diplomatic agent of the highest rank accredited to a foreign government or sovereign as the resident representative of his or her own government. Second Corinthians 5:17 says, we *"are new creations in Christ."* Jesus said in John 15:19 (NKJV), *"If you were of this world, the world would love its own. Yet because you are not of this world, but I chose you out of the world, therefore the world hates you."* Once you are born again, you become a new creation. Not only do we belong to a new family, but we are now living under a new kingdom, the Kingdom of God, and living according to His principles.

We must gain the understanding that we are no longer sinners on the earth, just trying to do the best we can in hopes of not making God mad. Maybe now and then, we might do something to gain His approval. No, no, and no! If you are born again, you are not some old sinner just trying to do the best you can. You are a new person. Ephesians 2:10 says, *"For we are His workmanship, created in Christ Jesus for good works, which God prepared beforehand that we should walk in them."*

It is my hope that as you have read some of my real life experiences in this book, you have been inspired by them. I pray that inspiration turns to revelation and you see yourself as Jesus sees you. And finally, that you are motivated by faith to step out and do what God has called you to do as His ambassador, His minister of reconciliation. *"Now all things are of God, who has reconciled us to Himself through Jesus Christ, and has given us the ministry of reconciliation"* (2 Corinthians 5:18 NKJV).

ABOUT THE AUTHOR

TIM GRISHAM was saved at thirteen years of age and began sharing Christ with others but always felt intimidated and fearful. Then, in 1981 at age twenty-two everything changed! Tim has ministered in thirty three countries around the world and all across the United States. For the past thirty-eight years Tim has not only ministered to multitudes with the power of the gospel but has focused his ministry as an Evangelist to training others to walk free from fear and in the supernatural power of God.

To follow up with Tim, connect online at:

🌐 **GOYE.ORG**

✉ **TGM12345@AOL.COM**

Made in the USA
Columbia, SC
01 October 2021